STUFFED TOYS

STITCHED
TOYS

20 stunning but simple designs

KATE HAXELL

hamlyn

An Hachette UK Company
www.hachette.co.uk

First published in Great Britain in 2009
by Hamlyn, a division of Octopus Publishing Group Ltd
Endeavour House, 189 Shaftesbury Avenue, London,
WC2H 8JY
www.octopusbooks.co.uk

ISBN 978-0-600-62384-7

A CIP catalogue record for this book is available from the
British Library.

Printed and bound in China

10 9 8 7 6 5 4 3 2 1

If a toy is for a baby, do not sew anything onto it that could be
pulled off and swallowed. Make sure that all seams are well
finished so stuffing cannot be pulled out. Babies must always
be supervised when playing with toys.

CONTENTS

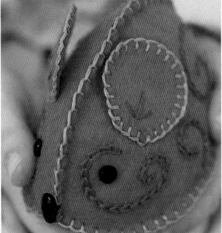

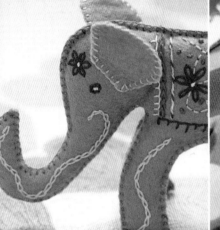

INTRODUCTION

Making toys is such great fun: they are small, quick to sew and you can let your creative flair run riot. If you are not a confident sewer, then a simple toy is the perfect project for you. The recipients of your efforts will not be critical of wobbly seams or mismatched eyes; they will love the toy for its character and because it was made especially for them.

The toys in this book range from super-simple felt mice (see Three Mice, page 44) to a richly embroidered doll (see Flower Doll, page 112). There are projects to do by hand (such as the Patchwork Gonk, page 54), and projects made almost entirely on the sewing machine (such as the Sausage Dog, page 108).

For every project, the required quantities and types of materials are given together with colour suggestions, but of course you can make your toy in whatever colour scheme you choose. You can also make the toys bigger or smaller than those here; simply enlarge the templates by a different percentage and adapt the materials accordingly.

I hope you have as much fun making these toys as I did.

Kate Haxell

EQUIPMENT

You don't need any special equipment to start making toys, just a few sewing basics. Always read through the equipment list at the start of each project to check that you have everything you need. It is very frustrating having to stop halfway through a project because you are missing something vital.

Scissors

A good pair of fabric scissors is essential, and a small pair of sharp embroidery scissors will be useful for cutting out detailed pattern pieces, for clipping curves and trimming seam allowances (see Finishing a seam, page 12). Don't use your fabric scissors for cutting out paper templates as paper will blunt the blades: use household or craft scissors instead.

Needles

You will need sewing needles and sewing threads. A good-size needle for sewing is a 10 sharp: it's tiny, so it slips easily through even the finest fabrics without leaving a hole. If you are good at hand-sewing, you can make toys entirely by hand. However, a sewing machine will save time in sewing longer seams. A machine with basic functions – straight stitch and zigzag stitch – is adequate for all of the toys in this book. Embroidery needles and threads are used in many of the projects.

Iron

You will need an iron for a number of the projects and your ordinary one will be fine. However, the tiny craft irons sold for appliqué and patchwork are useful for awkward corners.

When making the toys in this book, before turning a piece right side out, press it carefully.

Once you have turned it, press it again. If the piece is very small and you find it difficult to press accurately, then press the seams firmly with your fingers to coax them flat before carefully pressing with an iron.

Fabric markers

You will need some method of marking the fabric in order to make many of these toys. Use a specialist marker for this, not a pencil or writing pen. A fading fabric marker is ideal. These are a type of felt-tip pen with special ink that fades away after a time. If you find that the marks fade too quickly, try a water-soluble fabric marker. These are similar to a fading fabric marker, but the mark disappears when you wet it. Always test a marker on the fabric you are going to use to check that it fades away completely and/or that water doesn't spoil the fabric.

Embroidery hoop

Essential for embroidering details onto fabric, an embroidery hoop is used to keep the fabric taut while you are working.

USING AN EMBROIDERY HOOP

Lay the fabric over the inner hoop then open the screw on the outer hoop and slip it over the inner one, being careful not to pull the

fabric and distort the drawn design. Tighten the screw with a little screwdriver until it is as tight as possible. If you need to re-tension the fabric, don't pull on the edges of it, but release the screw and start again.

Fusible webbing

A great product for toy making, fusible webbing is a very thin sheet of heat-activated glue on a paper backing.

USING FUSIBLE WEBBING

The glue side of the sheet feels slightly rough; this is the side that you iron onto the fabric. It does stiffen the fabric quite a lot so don't use it on anything that you want to feel soft. Always read the manufacturer's directions on the pack you buy and follow them carefully. Press the iron in position; don't move it back and forth. If you get the webbing the wrong way up, you will iron it onto the soleplate of the iron, which makes a nasty mess that is difficult to clean off. If you are doing lots of toy making (or other crafts), then it may be worth buying a cheap iron just for fusible webbing.

Remember that if you are drawing around a template onto the paper backing of fusible webbing, you need to place the template right side down to ensure that the cut-out fabric piece will be the right way around.

MATERIALS

One of the great things about making toys is that they are small and so they don't need much fabric. This means you can raid your scrap bag and recycle clothes, curtains and more to make something lovely. Always keep a stash of potential fabric pieces, buying them when you see them; one day they will be perfect for a project you are working on.

Fabrics

Buying fabrics in shops is not the most economical way of purchasing toy fabric, as you can usually only buy a minimum of 20 cm (8 in) of the full width of a fabric when you may only need a 10 cm (4 in) square for any given project. Recycling a much-loved but outgrown child's dress or shirt for a toy for that child is more practical and a great way of personalizing the project. Hunt in second-hand shops and garage sales for garments that can be recycled (save buttons and trimmings as well as fabric). Avoid non-washable fabrics, although stains can usually be cut around.

Consider the size of the pattern on a fabric, which can be too big for the scale of a toy; children's garments with smaller patterns are useful. A good supply of small quantities of fabric, often with small-scale patterns, are the fat quarters sold for patchwork. Suppliers can be found on the internet (see page 128).

Trimmings

As with fabrics, you only need small quantities of embellishments. Shops will usually sell you as little as 10 cm (4 in), and interesting trimmings can be found in second-hand shops. Again, look for pieces with a small-scale pattern.

TECHNIQUES

You really don't need to be a skilled sewer to make the toys in this book. Basic hand and embroidery stitches will see most projects through to successful completion. There is a list of the techniques used at the beginning of each project, and it is worth reading through them here to make sure you know exactly what is required before starting the work.

Skill levels

It can be quite difficult to assess the difficulty of a project as what one person may find hard, another thinks is easy. However, you will find a number on each project giving it a skill level between 1 and 5. Projects rated 1 are great for novice toy makers while those rated 5 will please keen sewers.

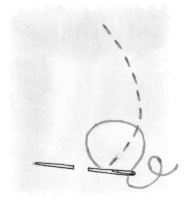

Running stitch

Hand-sewing techniques

Sewing by hand is one of the most satisfying crafts. It's portable, easy to do and you will always delight in seeing something you have made with your own hands. If you are new to hand-sewing, practise the stitches on scraps of fabric before starting a project.

RUNNING STITCH

The most basic of hand stitches, this is used for basting (see below), gathering and as an embroidery stitch.

Bring the needle up through the fabric at the start of the planned line of sewing. *Take it down a short distance away and bring it up again a short distance further along the line. Repeat from *.

BASTING

Basting simply uses running stitches to hold two or more fabrics together securely while you sew a seam. It is much easier to machine accurately if the fabrics are basted. Pinning isn't as good, as the pins lift the fabric a little when you put them in and you have to take them out before the sewing machine reaches them. Basting stitches don't have to be even or neat, as you take them out after sewing the seam.

BACKSTITCH

This stitch is used for hand-sewing very small seams or for sewing around tight curves that would be tricky to sew accurately with a sewing machine. You can also use it as an embroidery stitch.

Bring the needle up through the fabric a stitch-length beyond the start of the planned line of sewing. Take it back to the start of the line and down through the fabric. Bring it up a stitch-length beyond where it first came out. *Take it back down at the end of the last stitch and bring it up through the fabric a stitch-length beyond where it last came out. Repeat from *.

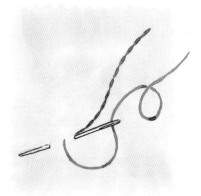

Backstitch

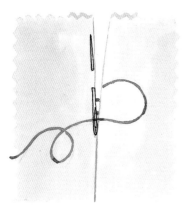

Ladder stitch

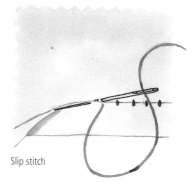

Slip stitch

LADDER STITCH

This stitch is used for invisibly closing a gap in a seam, usually once a toy has been turned right side out and stuffed. Ensure the seam allowances across the gap are pressed under by the correct amount before you start sewing.

Knot one end of the thread. Slip the needle into the gap in the seam and bring it out through the fabric on the folded edge of the seam allowance at the start of the gap. Pull the needle and thread through so that the knot is hidden on the inside. *Taking the needle straight across the gap, make a tiny stitch through the folded edge of the seam allowance on the other side and pull the needle and thread through. Go back to the first side and make a tiny stitch through the folded edge of the seam allowance, taking the needle straight across the gap. Pull the needle and thread through. The stitches should look like the rungs of a ladder spanning the gap. Repeat from *. After a few stitches, pull the thread tight to close the gap. The stitches should then be invisible.

SLIP STITCH

This is a hemming stitch that is almost invisible on the right side of the fabric. Turn under and press the hem before you start sewing.

Knot one end of the thread. From the back, take the needle through the folded-up hem, close to the edge, and pull the needle and thread through so that the knot is hidden behind the hem. *Take a tiny stitch through the main fabric, picking up just a couple of threads of it. Slide the point of the needle along between the hem and the main fabric and bring it out through the hem. Repeat from *.

OVERSEWING

Used for joining edges on the right or wrong side of the work, this is a simple and useful stitch. On the right side the stitches are visible, but that would be part of the effect. The stitches hardly show on the wrong side. If the edges to be joined have pressed-under seam allowances, then the stitches can be worked very close to the edge. However, if the fabric is felt, make the stitches a short distance from the edge or they will pull through it and the seam will split.

Baste the edges together before you start oversewing the seam. Knot one end of the thread and take it through the fabric from the wrong to the right side at the start of the seam. *Take the needle over the top of the edges of the fabric then take it straight through both of them, as close to the edge as needed. Pull the needle and thread through. Repeat from *.

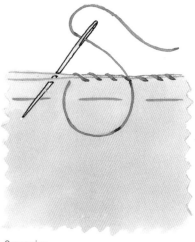

Oversewing

Sewing a seam

If you are new to sewing there are a couple of things you can do to make your seams smoother and neater.

If you are hand-sewing the seam, mark the sewing line on the fabric using a fabric marker (see page 8). It's easier to keep the line of sewing straight or create a smoothly curved line if you have something to follow.

Don't pull the stitches too tight: you may think you should to make the seam neat but gentle tension is enough. If you pull the stitches too tight the seam will unattractively pucker.

If you are machine-sewing the seam, the golden rule is to take your time; press the peddle gently and sew slowly. The machine will pull the fabric through at the required rate, so concentrate on guiding it in under the needle, not pulling it through. Remember to keep your fingers well away from the needle.

Always machine-sew a couple of scraps of the fabric together before you start the project to check that the stitch tension is right; consult your machine manual for instructions on altering this if need be.

Either line the edge of the fabric up with the appropriate mark on the machine plate and keep an eye on it so that the line of sewing is always the same distance from the edge of the fabric, or mark the line as for hand-sewing.

Finishing a seam

Once you have sewn a seam, by hand or by machine, you need to finish it neatly so that it is secure and looks good.

If you are hand-sewing, knot the thread to start the sewing. To secure the thread, make a few tiny backstitches in the seam allowance, next to the line of stitching.

If you are machine-sewing, reverse a few stitches at the beginning and end of the seam to secure the threads. Refer to your sewing machine manual to see how to do this. Alternatively, pull both threads through to one side of the fabric and tie them in a secure double knot.

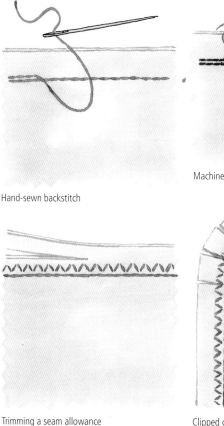

Hand-sewn backstitch

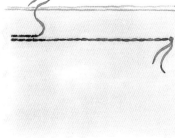

Machine-sewing

Seams on small items, such as toys, will look better if they are trimmed. Cut off any excess fabric about 5 mm (¼ in) from the line of sewing. If the fabric you are using frays a lot or if the seam will be under strain, then zigzag stitch on the machine within the seam allowance, close to the seam line. Trim excess fabric close to the zigzag stitching.

To make curved seams lie flat, you need to clip them. Do this after zigzagging and trimming the seam allowance. Using small, sharp scissors, cut little notches around the curved section of the seam. Cut almost up to the seam line of sewing.

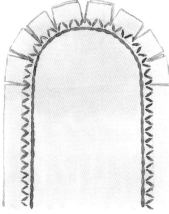

Trimming a seam allowance

Clipped curved seam

Embroidery techniques

The secret of successful embroidery is practice. None of the stitches used in this book are difficult to do, but if you are a novice embroiderer, it is a good idea to practise the stitches needed for your project before you work on the toy itself.

Use a leftover piece of the same fabric and the correct threads and work the stitches until you are happy with the results. Don't pull the embroidery stitches too tight or they will become distorted and will pucker the fabric. You need just enough tension for them to lie flat and smooth.

Use a small knot to secure the thread on the back of the fabric at the start of the sewing. When you have finished, take the needle through to the back again and secure it by looping it under the back of a stitch, taking the needle through the loop and pulling the resulting knot tight. Make a couple of these knots to hold the end firmly and do not trim the thread too close to the last knot.

BLANKET STITCH

You can work blanket stitch on a piece of fabric or over the edge of it, making the 'legs' even or uneven in length. It only takes a little practice to get into the rhythm of this stitch and you will be able to judge the leg length and spacing of the stitches to achieve a neat result.

To work the stitch on fabric (1) bring the needle through from the back. *Take the needle into the fabric at the top of a leg and bring the point out at the bottom of the leg. Loop the working yarn under the point of the needle and pull the needle through the fabric. Pull on the thread to tighten the stitch. Repeat from *.

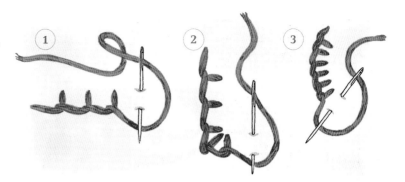

Blanket stitch

To work the stitch over the edge of fabric bring the needle through from the back. *Take the point of the needle down through the fabric at the required distance from the edge. Loop the working thread under the point (as for working the stitch on fabric – see above), pull the needle through the fabric and tighten the stitch. Repeat from *.

To work the stitch around a right-angled corner (2), space the stitches so that the last one on the first side is about a stitched leg's-length from the corner. Make the next stitch a diagonal one across the corner, inserting the needle next to the leg of the previous stitch. Now insert the needle next to the leg of the diagonal stitch to make the first straight stitch on the second side.

To work the stitch around a curve (3), angle the legs so that the stitches run smoothly along the curve.

CHAIN STITCH

Used for embroidering many of the faces in these projects, you can work this stitch in straight lines, tight spirals and any shape in between.

Bring the needle up through the fabric at the start of the planned line of sewing. Take it back down next to where it came up *and bring the point up a short distance away. Loop the working thread under the point and pull the needle and thread through. Take the needle down next to where it last came out and repeat from *.

Chain stitch

Feather stitch

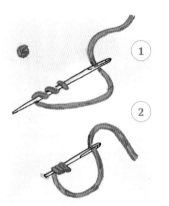

French knot

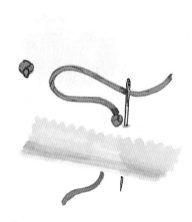

Fake French knot

FEATHER STITCH

You can work this decorative stitch in straight lines or gentle curves. You can make the 'legs' on both sides, as shown, or on one side only, by making the straight stitch from the same side down to the centre each time.

Bring the needle up through the fabric at the top centre of the planned line of sewing. *Take the needle down through the fabric to the right and on the same level as where it came out and make a short, diagonal stitch to the centre. Loop the working thread under the point and pull the needle through. Pull gently on the thread to tighten the stitch. Take the needle down through the fabric to the left and on the same level as where it came out and make a short, diagonal stitch to the centre. Loop the working thread under the point and pull the needle through and tighten the stitch. Repeat from *.

FRENCH KNOT

These are useful for embroidering nostrils and pupils for eyes on dolls' faces and for making centres for flowers.

1 Bring the needle up through the fabric at the required position of the knot and pull the thread through. Holding the needle flat next to where it came out, wind the thread around the needle three times.

2 Put your left thumb over the coils on the needle and pull the needle backwards until the coils are close to the point. Now take the needle down through the fabric, slowly and close to where it came out, pulling both needle and thread through the coils. Keep your left thumb over the coils until the knot is pulled tight.

FAKE FRENCH KNOT

Sometimes it can be tricky to work a French knot in the centre of an eye or flower without catching existing embroidery. In these instances you can use this cheat's version, which is indistinguishable from the real thing.

Tie a knot the required size about 10 cm (4 in) from one end of a length of thread. Thread this end into a needle and take it down through the fabric where you want the knot to sit. Take the needle off the thread and thread it with the opposite end. Take this end down through the fabric next to the knot. Turn the fabric over and pull gently on the ends so that the knot sits flat against the right side. Knot the ends securely on the back to finish.

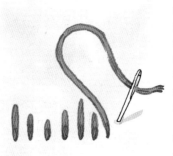

Lazy daisy stitch

Stab stitch (straight stitch)

LAZY DAISY STITCH

This is primarily used for making flowers. These can have as many petals as you want; for the perfect five-petal flower, turn to Cool Cat, page 58.

1 *Bring the needle up through the fabric in the centre of the planned flower. Take it back down next to where it came up, bringing the point up a short distance away (at the tip of the petal). Loop the working thread under the point and pull the needle and thread through.

2 Now take the needle over the end of the loop and back down through the fabric to hold the loop in position. Repeat from *.

STAB STITCH

Also known as straight stitch, this simply involves making straight stitches of the required length where needed.

Bring the needle up through the fabric and take it back down the required distance away.

WHIPPED STITCHES

Running stitch, backstitch and chain stitch can all be 'whipped' – which you can do in one of two ways depending on the effect you want – using the same colour thread or a contrast colour. The steps shown here are on running stitch.

Bring the needle up through the fabric at the start of the line of stitches to be whipped (1). *Without catching the fabric, take the needle upwards under the first stitch. Take it downwards under the next stitch. Repeat from *.

Alternatively, bring the needle up through the fabric at the start of the line of stitches to be whipped (2). *Without catching the fabric, take the needle downwards under the first stitch. Then take it downwards under the next stitch. Repeat from *.

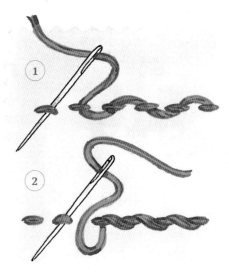

Whipped stitches

Creating a face

Embroider the eyes first, as these are usually the hardest parts of the face to get right. Above all, take your time. Don't do this part of a doll in a hurry or in front of a distracting television programme. The thing to avoid is making the eyes look too staring. There are a few tricks you can use to avoid this:

• Unless the doll has black hair or very dark skin, do not use black to embroider the eyes; dark-brown is better.

• Do not make the eyes a complete oval shape; all the dolls in this book have a little gap at the inner corner of the eye.

• Use more than one shade of a colour to embroider the pupil. For instance, work an outer circle in one colour then fill in the middle of it in a lighter shade (see Dress-up Doll, page 32 and left).

• It always pays to work a practice eye before starting the actual project. Use the same fabrics and threads and take the opportunity to experiment and see what looks best.

• Unless you are a skilled embroiderer, avoid using backstitch for features. It makes a hard line and it's difficult to keep the stitches really straight and even. Use whipped backstitch or chain stitch (see pages 10, 13 and 15) instead for a softer, more forgiving line.

Creating a face

For some projects in this book you will cut the features out of a template and draw around them onto the head. For others, you will need to transfer the outlines of facial features onto the fabric using a water-soluble or fading fabric marker (see page 8). Make sure that they are as symmetrical as possible before embroidering them following the instructions in the project and always use an embroidery hoop (see page 8).

As you embroider, resist the temptation to unpick and redo your work unless you have made a really bad mistake: you will forever be unpicking and will spoil both the fabric and the thread. If you do decide to unpick, take the time to look at the work first and decide what it is you need to do to improve it. If you are unpicking just a couple of stitches, take the thread out of the needle and use the eye end of the needle to unpick the stitches carefully. Don't use the point, as you may catch the fabric threads and pull them. If you are unpicking a whole section, very carefully cut the stitches with small, sharp scissors, and use tweezers to pull out any strands.

Making hair

Always give a doll plenty of hair; a skimpy covering will not look good. You can buy dolls' hair fibres in specialist doll-making shops, but it is pleasing to use knitting yarn, tapestry wool or embroidery threads for a more toy-like look. The thickness of the yarn will depend on the scale of the doll, but generally a double-knitting-weight yarn will work well. Embroidery threads should only be used on small dolls.

To make curly hair (see Dress-up Doll, page 32), knit up the yarn first. Use knit stitch only and just knit a square or rectangle. Do not cast the stitches off, just slip them off the needle. Following the manufacturer's instructions, press the knitting. Leave it to cool, then press it again and leave it to cool. Unravel the yarn and use it to make the hairstyle you want.

Hair can be made of just one colour of yarn or in varying shades of a colour to create a highlighted effect. You could also try using bright pinks or purples for a punk-style doll.

Yarn with distinct plies can be untwisted to make frizzy hair, but do test the process first on a short length of the chosen yarn: not all yarns untwist well and the results can look odd.

Iron embroidery thread before using it, to remove the hard kinks caused by it having been in a skein. To make very fine hair, separate the strands once you have sewn them on (see Flower Doll, page 112). Don't try and comb yarn or thread hair out with a hair comb before styling it, try using a table fork instead.

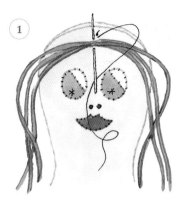

Centre parting

CENTRE PARTING

Cut strands of yarn twice as long as you want the finished hair, plus 2.5 cm (1 in). Sew the strands on in groups of three or four at a time. If you use larger numbers of strands they won't be attached very securely and may pull out.

1 Thread a hand-sewing needle with a long length of sewing thread in a colour to match the yarn you are using and knot one end. Make a small stitch through the doll's forehead, bringing the needle out where you want the hair to start. Lay the first group of strands over the forehead just below where the thread comes out, making sure they hang down to

Side parting

roughly the same length on either side of the face. Make a small backstitch (see page 10) over the strands, bringing the needle out a short distance further up the forehead. Pull the stitch tight.

2 Repeat the process, sewing up over the crown and at least halfway down the back of the head to attach as many groups of yarn as needed. Secure the thread through the head fabric between the last two groups of strands. When you have attached the hair to the top of the head, style it (see page 18) and trim it to the desired length.

SIDE PARTING

You work this in the same way as a centre parting (see above), but you start the stitching on one side of the head. As you attach groups of strands, angle the line of sewing so that by the time you reach the crown, the stitches are in the middle of the head. Stitch the groups of strands to the back of the head in a straight line down the middle. You will need to position the groups of strands so that the hair is an even length on each side of the parting all around the head. When you have attached the hair, style it (see page 18) and trim it to the desired length.

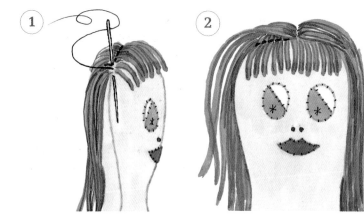

Fringe

FRINGE

To make a fringe, cut strands of yarn the length of the hair down the back of the head, plus the length of the fringe, plus 2.5 cm (1 in).

1 Thread a hand-sewing needle with a long length of sewing thread in a colour to match the yarn you are using and knot one end. Make a stitch through the seam on the crown of the head on the right-hand side of where you want the hair to start. Lay a group of strands over the crown, to the right of the thread and positioned so that the fringe hangs a little longer than the desired finished length.

Backstitch (see page 10) over the strands as for a centre parting (see page 17), sewing along the crown seam. Secure the thread through the head fabric between the last two groups of strands.

2 This alone will not give the doll enough hair, so you will need to add more on top of the fringe using a centre or side parting technique (see page 17). Usually you will want to start the parting further back than normal to allow the fringe to show.

STYLING HAIR

Even if you wish to leave the hair loose, you need to secure it so that it stays neat and tidy. You may also wish to style it further by making bunches or plaits.

For hair that hangs evenly all around the head, thread a needle as for a centre parting. Take the needle through the side seam at ear level (if the doll had ears) and bring it through the face where you want the edge of the hair to hang. Make backstitches (see page 10) over groups of three or four strands of yarn hair, working around the head at the same level. Secure the thread under the hair at the centre back and start the process again on the other side of the face.

To make bunches, divide the hair into two sections, one on either side of the face. Sew the hair in place as above, but sew over groups of eight or ten strands so that the strands do not spread around to the back of the head.

Plaits can be made by sewing bunches and then plaiting the hair below them. You can sew small motifs to hair for hair accessories, such as flowers at the tops of bunches (see Pocket Doll, page 48).

Styling hair

Stuffing a toy

All of the toys in this book are stuffed with polyester toy stuffing. Child-safe and washable, this is an excellent stuffing material, though there are a few things to note:

• Polyester stuffing tends to clump up a bit, so when you pull a piece from the bag, stretch it out and fluff it up with your fingers before stuffing it into the toy. Use a lot of small pieces to stuff toys, not two or three large lumps.

• Don't poke the stuffing in using something sharp, such as the tips of scissors or a metal knitting needle: you risk pushing right through the stuffing and damaging the toy you have almost completed. Use a blunt object instead, such as the handle of a teaspoon or the head of a knitting needle.

• For stuffing very tiny areas, such as a doll's thumb, use the tip of a bamboo knitting needle (they are blunter than metal needles) and use it with caution.

Project instructions will say how firmly a toy should be stuffed. If it is to be stuffed lightly, use just enough stuffing for the toy to hold its shape. The toy should feel soft and squashy. If it is to be stuffed firmly, then you need to pack the stuffing in, but not so tightly that the shape of the toy is distorted. Be careful if stuffing a felt toy firmly; felt stretches and you may burst the stitches.

Washing toys

If you use a washable stuffing (see left) and washable fabrics, there is no reason why you shouldn't be able to hand-wash your toy. However, don't risk putting it in the washing machine. Use a gentle detergent and soak the toy in warm soapy water then gently squeeze it. Avoid rubbing embroidery or button or bead embellishments. Don't wring out the toy, instead peg it to a clothesline and let it drip dry.

PLAYTIME

GLOVE PUPPETS

Made from non-fraying felt and decorated with simple embroidery stitches, these character puppets are quick and easy to make. Enlarge the templates as required to fit any size of hand and flip them over to make right- or left-handed versions.

MATERIALS

For the owl:

Paper for template

Two pieces of brown felt large enough to accommodate template

Scraps of pale-brown, bright-orange, orange-yellow and pale-orange felt

Brown, orange-yellow and variegated orange-to-yellow stranded embroidery threads

For the girl:

Paper for template

One piece each of white and yellow felt large enough to accommodate template

Scraps of yellow and pale-blue felt

Brown, pale-blue, pale-pink and yellow stranded embroidery threads

Three purchased flower motifs or flowers cut from trimming

EQUIPMENT

Owl and girl templates, page 116

Paper scissors

Fading fabric marker

Fabric scissors

Fabric glue

Embroidery needle

Small, sharp scissors

TECHNIQUES

Embroidery techniques, page 13–15

To make the owl

1 Use a photocopier to enlarge the template to the required size onto a piece of paper: it needs to be big enough to fit the child's hand without stretching the felt. Cut the template out.

2 Use the fabric marker to draw around the whole hand shape onto both pieces of brown felt and cut out two hands. Cut the wings, outer eyes and beak out of the template. Draw around the wings onto pale-brown felt, the outer eyes onto bright-orange and the beak onto orange-yellow. Cut the inner eyes out of the template and draw around them onto pale-orange felt. Cut out all the shapes.

Getting it right

The fabric glue is just to hold the pieces in place while you sew them, so you really do only need a few tiny dabs of it. Too much glue will stiffen the felt and stop the puppet moving easily.

3 Apply a few small dabs of fabric glue to the thumb of one of the brown hands and stick the pale-brown thumb wing to it, aligning the tops of the thumb shapes. Apply a few dabs of glue to the other wing and stick it to the other side of the hand, following the template. Using the embroidery needle and three strands of brown thread, work running stitch (see page 10) right around the thumb, sewing through both layers close to, but not right on, the edge of the pale-brown felt. Work running stitch around the inner edge of the other wing in the same way.

4 Apply a dab of glue to the backs of the inner eyes and lay them centrally on the outer eyes. Using three strands of orange-yellow thread, work blanket stitch (see page 13) around the edges of the inner eyes. Using the small, sharp scissors, cut the outer eyes into points.

5 Apply dabs of glue to the backs of the central part of the eyes and stick them to the brown hand. Using three strands of brown, work a line of running stitch on the outer eyes, around the edge of the inner eyes, to sew the eyes to the hand. Using small stab stitches (see page 15), work brown stars for the pupils.

6 Apply a dab of glue to the back of the beak and stick it to the brown hand. Using three strands of orange-yellow thread, work blanket stitch around the beak.

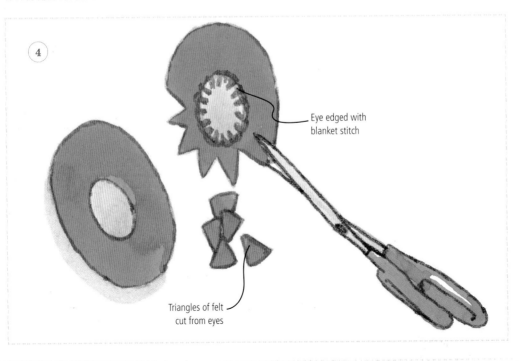

Eye edged with blanket stitch

Triangles of felt cut from eyes

Wing lifted
forward

Needle working
blanket stitch

7 Wrong sides facing, lay the two hand shapes together. Using three strands of variegated orange-to-yellow thread and starting at the bottom of the thumb, work blanket stitch right around the hands to join them. When stitching around the thumb, lift the edge of the wing forward so that you don't catch it in the stitching. Continue stitching around the hand, catching the edge of the other wing in the blanket stitches. Stitch around the base of the glove.

To make the girl

1 Use a photocopier to enlarge the template to the required size onto a piece of paper: it needs to be big enough to fit the child's hand without stretching the felt. Cut the template out.

2 Use the fabric marker to draw around the whole hand shape onto the pieces of white and yellow felt and cut out one hand in each colour. Cut the hair and dress out of the template. Draw around the hair onto yellow felt and the dress onto pale-blue felt. Cut out the shapes.

3 Cut the features out of the template and draw around them onto the white hand. Using the embroidery needle and two strands of thread, embroider the features. Starting at the lower inner corner of the eyes, embroider the outlines in brown chain stitch (see page 13). Work concentric circles of pale-blue chain stitch for the irises and brown French knots (see page 14) for the pupils. Work brown French knots for the nostrils. Outline the mouth in pink chain stitch and fill it in with more concentric lines of the same stitch.

4 Apply a few dabs of fabric glue to the back of the hair section and stick it to the white hand, following the template. Using three strands of yellow thread, work chain stitch close to, but not right on, the edge of the yellow felt, around the inner edge of the hair and around the curl on the thumb. Work a line of yellow backstitch (see page 10) to define the parting.

5 Apply a few dabs of fabric glue to the back of the dress and stick it to the white hand. Using three strands of pale-blue thread, work a line of running stitch (see page 10) around the side and top edges of the dress.

6 Wrong sides facing, lay the two hand shapes together. Using three strands of yellow thread and starting at the bottom of the thumb, work blanket stitch right around the hands to join them. Stitch around the base of the glove.

7 Apply fabric glue to the backs of the flower motifs and stick them to the puppet, using the photograph as a guide.

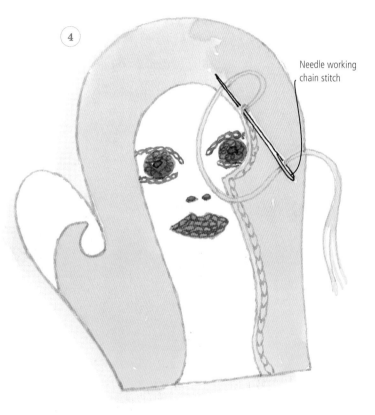

Needle working
chain stitch

PLAY CUBES

Baby-friendly and practical, these cubes can be customized to suit any nursery. Make them in the same fabric as the nursery curtains (as long as it's washable) for a perfectly coordinated toy.

MATERIALS
For each cube:
Paper for template
Scraps of main fabrics
Six 12 cm (5 in) squares of
 medium-weight fabric, such as
 ticking
Sewing threads to match and
 contrast with fabrics
10 cm (4 in) cube of firm foam

EQUIPMENT
Heart template, page 116
Paper scissors
Iron

Fusible webbing
Fading fabric marker
Fabric scissors
Pair of compasses
Sewing machine
Pins
Thin knitting needle
Hand-sewing needle

TECHNIQUES
Using fusible webbing, page 8
Hand-sewing techniques,
 pages 10–12
Finishing a seam, page 12

Choosing fabrics
If you are using patterned or striped fabrics, consider the placement of the pattern when cutting both the squares for the cube and the appliqué motifs. Arrange stripes so that they run symmetrically across squares. If you are using highly patterned fabrics, you may prefer not to appliqué motifs to them at all.

1 Use a photocopier to enlarge the template to the desired size onto a piece of paper and cut it out. It needs to be small enough to fit into a 10 cm (4 in) square. Iron fusible webbing onto the back of a scrap of fabric (see page 8). Lay the heart template on the right side of the fabric and draw around it with the fabric marker. Cut out the heart, peel off the paper backing and iron it onto a 12 cm (5 in) square of fabric, ensuring that a seam allowance of at least 1 cm (½ in) is left free around the edges of the square.

2 Iron fusible webbing onto more scraps of fabric. Using the compasses, draw circles of varying diameters onto the paper backings. Cut out the circles, peel off the backings and iron the circles onto fabric squares, leaving seam allowances free as in Step 1. Not every square needs to have a motif, only as many as you wish.

3 Thread the sewing machine with contrast thread and set it to a narrow, tight zigzag stitch. If your sewing machine has a specific satin-stitch function, then use that. Working slowly and carefully, zigzag-stitch around the motifs.

4 Right sides facing, pin two squares together along one edge. Thread the machine with thread to match the fabric and set it to a medium straight stitch. Taking a 1 cm (½ in) seam allowance, sew the squares together along the pinned edge. Remove the pins, open the squares out and press the seam allowance open. It is important to take accurate seam allowances throughout and to sew in straight lines for a neatly finished cube.

5 On one of the joined squares, right sides facing, pin the edge opposite the seamed edge to another square. Sew the seam and press it as in Step 4. Repeat until you have sewn four squares together to make a strip measuring 42 x 12 cm (17 x 5 in).

6 Right sides facing, pin one of the remaining squares to a free edge of the second square in the strip. Sew the seam as before, but start and stop the stitching 1 cm (½ in) from the edges of the new square, in alignment with the already-sewn seams. Sew the last square of fabric to the opposite edge of the second square in the same way. The result should be a cross shape.

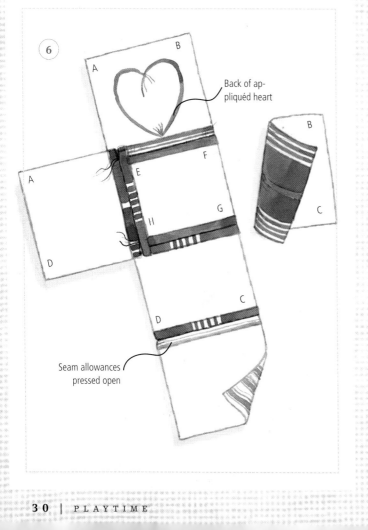

Back of ap-pliquéd heart

Seam allowances pressed open

Getting it right

Satin-stitch machine-appliqué does take a bit of practice, so if you haven't done it before, test your technique on scraps of fabric before starting the project. For hearts, start sewing at the bottom of the V in the top of the heart. To work around curves, stop stitching with the needle down in the fabric on the outside edge of the line of satin stitch. Raise the presser foot, turn the fabric just a little then lower the foot and sew a few more stitches. Repeat this to go right around a curve, or circle, neatly. Finish the line of sewing at the bottom of the heart, pull the threads through to the back and knot them securely. Sew the other side of the heart, starting at the bottom of the V again.

7 Following the illustration opposite, pin marked point A to corresponding marked point A. Sew the seam, starting 1 cm (½ in) from the open end and stopping when you reach the previous seam line at E. Repeat the process to sew B to B, stopping at F; C to C, stopping at G and D to D, stopping at H. You will have made a box with one open side that has a square sewn to one edge of it, like a flap. Press under a 1 cm (½ in) seam allowance around the three raw edges of this flap.

8 Fit the foam cube into the box. It should fit tightly, so you will need to wriggle and ease the fabric over it. Slip the knitting needle into the cube along the edges and use it to 'stroke' the seam allowances down over the edges of the foam cube. It isn't vital that all the allowances lie perfectly flat, but it will help give the cube a neat finish.

9 Fold 1 cm (½ in) of the edges of the squares around the open side of the box over the foam. Pin the pressed-under edges of the flap to the folded edges of the box, making the seams as neat and straight as possible. Using the hand-sewing needle and matching thread, ladder stitch (see page 11) the seams to complete the cube.

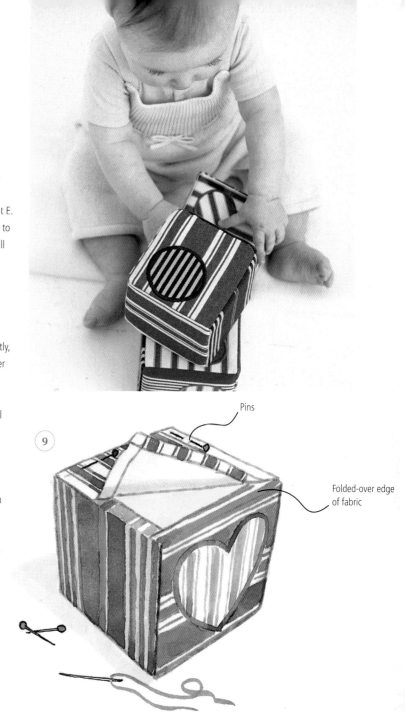

Pins

Folded-over edge of fabric

DRESS-UP DOLL

This pretty doll comes with patterns for a dress, jacket and shoes that you can alter and embellish to create unique outfits. You do need sewing skills for this project, but she's well worth the effort.

MATERIALS

Paper for templates

Two 30 x 15 cm (12 x 6 in), four 28 x 10 cm (11 x 4 in) and four 17 x 6 cm (6¾ x 2½ in) pieces of medium-weight, pale-brown cotton fabric

Dark-brown, dark-olive-green, olive-green, dark-red and variegated pink stranded embroidery threads

Sewing threads in pale-brown, dark-brown and to match garment fabrics

Toy stuffing

Basting thread

Seed beads to tone with garment fabrics

Approximately 15 g (½ oz) of DK-weight dark-brown knitting yarn

Butterfly motifs or motifs cut from trimming

Two 23 cm (9 in) squares of plain cotton dress fabric

1 m (1 yd) of narrow bias binding to tone with plain cotton dress fabric

Two small poppers

Two 30 x 12 cm (12 x 4¾ in) pieces of printed cotton jacket fabric

Two 8 cm (3 in) squares and two 8 x 4 cm (3 x 1½ in) pieces of felt

Five small buttons

EQUIPMENT

Dress-up doll templates, page 117

Paper scissors

Fading fabric marker

10 cm (4 in) embroidery hoop

Hand-sewing and beading needles

Sewing machine

Pins

Knitting needles the size recommended on the yarn ball band

TECHNIQUES

Using an embroidery hoop, page 8

Hand-sewing techniques, pages 10–12

Finishing a seam, page 12

Creating a face, page 16

Making hair, page 17

Stuffing a toy, page 19

1 Photocopy the templates at 300 per cent onto pieces of paper and cut them out. Using the fabric marker, draw around the outer edge of the body onto both large pieces of brown cotton fabric. Cut out one of the shapes.

2 Fit the head area of the second body into the embroidery hoop (see page 8). Using the hand-sewing needle and one strand of embroidery thread, embroider the face. Outline the doll's eyes in dark-brown chain stitch (see page 13). Using tiny stitches and starting at the inner corner, embroider the upper eyelid then embroider the lower lid. Stop before you meet the inner corner of the eye again and finish with a long straight stitch (see page 15) holding the

last loop down. Use dark-brown lazy daisy stitches (see page 15), for the eyelashes, each with a long straight stitch holding the loop down. Using the same tiny chain stitch and dark-olive-green thread, embroider circles for the irises in the centre of each eye. Fill in these circles with a tightly coiled spiral of olive-green chain stitches. Work dark-brown French knots (see page 14) for the pupils and nostrils. Work the mouth in dark red chain-stitch and each cheek with a tightly coiled spiral of variegated pink, cutting the thread so that the circles start as pale pink and get darker towards the centre. When you have completed the embroidery, cut out the body shape.

3 Draw around the leg template onto the four 28 x 10 cm (11 x 4 in) pieces of cotton and the arm template onto the four 17 x 6 cm (6¾ x 2½ in) pieces. Set the sewing machine to a medium straight stitch and thread it with pale-brown thread. Right sides facing, and taking a 1 cm (½ in) seam allowance, machine-sew pairs of arms and legs together to make two arms and two legs, leaving the top edges open. You may find it easier to sew around the small thumbs by hand using backstitch (see page 10). Sew a narrow zigzag stitch just outside the seams, trim the seam allowances and clip the curves (see page 12). Turn right side out and press. Stuff the limbs lightly (see page 19) so that they remain floppy and baste the openings closed.

4 Work four lines of linked running stitch (see page 10) to define the fingers and thumb on each hand. Work tiny running stitches in one direction, sewing through all layers, and then work back in the opposite direction, filling in the gaps. On one hand, as you start the last line, sew on seed beads to make a ring on the ring finger. Secure the ends of the thread invisibly in the seam. Work a line of linked running stitch across each leg at the dotted line on the template to make a knee joint.

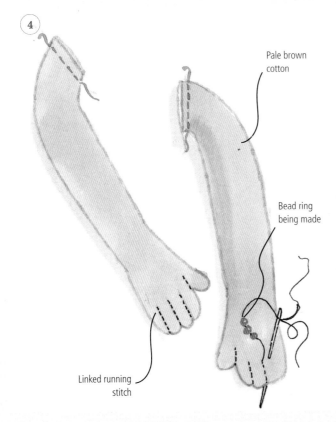

④

Pale brown cotton

Bead ring being made

Linked running stitch

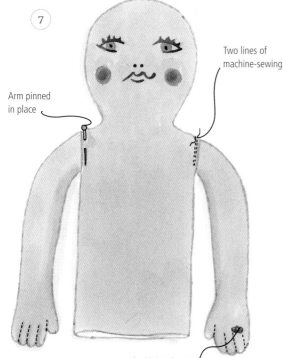

Arm pinned in place

Two lines of machine-sewing

Hand with bead ring

8 Reposition the pins so that the legs are pinned to the front part of the body only. Firmly stuff the head and body through the gap behind the legs. Re-pin the legs to both sides of the body, check they are still the same length, and then machine-sew across them as for the arms.

9 Knit the yarn up into a garter-stitch strip and press it. When the knitting is cold, unravel the yarn so you can make curly hair (see page 17). Cut 30 cm (12 in) lengths of yarn and make them into hair with a centre parting (see page 17). Sew the hair down around the head at ear level. Sew two butterflies to the hair as hair decorations.

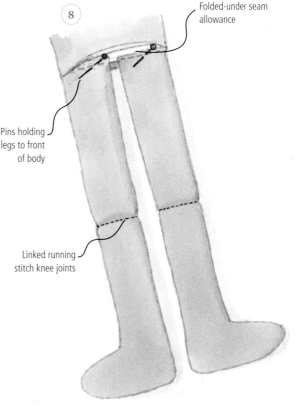

Folded-under seam allowance

Pins holding legs to front of body

Linked running stitch knee joints

5 Right sides facing, machine-sew the two body pieces together, starting and stopping at the dotted lines on the template to leave openings for the arms and legs. Zigzag the edges, trim seams and turn right side out and press, making sure that the seam allowances are pressed under at the openings.

6 Slip 1 cm (½ in) of each arm and leg into its opening and pin them in place. Make sure that the thumbs on the hands are next to the body to give you right and left arms. Make sure that both the arms and both the legs are the same lengths.

7 Machine-sew across the body where the arms enter it, sewing close to the edge of the body fabric. Sew over the line twice, reversing at each end of the line of sewing, to make sure the arms are firmly attached.

10 Draw around the whole dress template twice onto one square of plain cotton fabric. Cut out the shapes: these are the dress backs. Trim the template down to the inner solid line. Fold the remaining square of plain cotton fabric in half lengthways. Pin the dress template to it with the long straight edge against the fold. Draw around it and cut out the shape: this is the dress front.

11 Right sides facing, pin the dress backs together along the long straight edge. Thread the sewing machine with matching thread and machine-sew the backs together, taking a 1 cm (½ in) seam allowance. Start at the hem and stop 5 cm (2 in) from the neck. Zigzag the seam allowances separately. Press the seam allowance open, pressing under the allowance on the open section at the same time. Turn under the raw edge of the hem on the open section and slip stitch (see page 11) it in place.

Folded and slip stitched hem

Zigzagged seam allowance

(11)

12 Right sides facing, machine-sew the dress front and back together along the shoulder and side seams. Zigzag the edges and trim the seam allowances. Bind the neck, armholes and hem of the dress with bias binding. Sew a popper at the top of the opening in the back of the dress. Sew a butterfly to the hem on one side.

13 Fold one piece of printed cotton in half lengthways. Lay the jacket template against the fold and cut out one shape; this is the jacket back. Trim the template down to the inner solid lines. Draw around this shape twice onto the second piece of printed cotton and cut out the shapes: these are the jacket fronts. Right sides facing, pin the fronts to the back, aligning the sleeves. Machine-sew along the tops of the arms and the underarm and side seams. Zigzag the edges and trim the seam allowances. Press under a narrow double hem around all raw edges and slip stitch it in place. Sew the remaining popper on at the top of the front opening. Sew one button on to cover the back of the popper.

Dressing up

You can easily alter the garment patterns to create your own outfits. Keep the width of the dress the same and lengthen it, flaring the skirt out, to make an evening dress. Trim it with satin bias binding. Cut the pattern at the waist to make a tank top and use the skirt section to make an A-line skirt, adding a ribbon waistband fastened at the back with a popper. Shorten the jacket sleeves and body length to make a shrug or extend them to make a coat. There are lots of possibilities based on these simple patterns.

Side of shoe
with strap

(14)

Needle sewing
end of strap
to other side
of shoe

14 Draw around the shoe template onto the two larger squares of felt and cut out the shapes. Cut the strap off the template. Draw around the shoe onto the two smaller pieces of felt and cut out the shapes. Pair one strap shoe with one strapless shoe. Using the hand-sewing needle and matching sewing thread, sew the two pieces together with blanket stitch (see page 13). Continue the stitching around the top of the shoe and along the edges of the strap. Fold the end of the strap over and sew it to the strapless shoe. Sew a button over the end of the strap on both sides of the shoe. Make up the other shoe in the same way.

15 Thread seed beads onto lengths of thread to make a necklace and bracelet. Tie them around the doll's neck and wrist with firm double knots.

BEANBAGS

Made using simple appliqué and embroidery techniques, these three characters will appeal to all children and they do thoroughly enjoy being thrown about in the pursuit of fun.

MATERIALS
For the lion:
Paper for template
15.5 x 12 cm (6¼ x 4¾ in) piece of yellow chenille fabric
15.5 x 12 cm (6¼ x 4¾ in) piece of brown felt
Scrap of brown felt
Brown and black stranded embroidery threads
50 cm (20 in) of yellow furnishing fringe
Basting thread and yellow sewing thread
Dried lentils
Yellow perlé embroidery thread

For the pirate:
Paper for template
Two 13 x 9.5 cm (5 x 3¾ in) pieces of brown felt
9 x 9.5 cm (3½ x 3¾ in) piece of red felt
Scraps of white, black and green felt
White, red, black, green and brown sewing threads
Black and yellow stranded embroidery threads
Dried lentils

For the dog:
Paper for template
Two 15.5 x 12 cm (6¼ x 2½ in) and one 8 x 6 cm (3 x 2½ in) pieces of pale-brown needlecord fabric with the ridges running lengthways
One 7 x 8.5 cm (2¾ x 3¼ in) piece of dark-brown needlecord fabric with the ridges running widthways and one 8 x 6 cm (3 x 2½ in) piece with the ridges running lengthways
Dark-brown, white, black, red and pale-brown sewing threads
Scraps of white, black and red felt
Black stranded embroidery thread
Two 1-cm (½-in) diameter pale-blue buttons
Two 8 x 6 cm (3 x 2½ in) pieces of pale-brown cotton fabric
Dried lentils

EQUIPMENT
Lion, pirate and dog templates, page 117
Paper scissors
Fading fabric marker
Fabric scissors
Iron
Fusible webbing
Pencil
Embroidery and hand-sewing needles
Pins
Fabric glue
Sewing machine

TECHNIQUES
Using fusible webbing, page 8
Hand-sewing techniques, pages 10–12
Finishing a seam, page 12
Embroidery techniques, pages 13–16

4 Baste the fringe just inside the edge of the brown felt piece cut in Step 1, positioning it so that just the strands protrude from the edge.

5 Right side up, lay the face on top of the brown felt, aligning the edges. Pin and baste the layers together. Using the hand-sewing needle and yellow sewing thread, oversew (see page 11) the front and back together, stitching between the strands of fringe. This is a bit fiddly, but the beanbag isn't big so it doesn't take long. Before completing the sewing, half-fill the beanbag with dried lentils. Remove all basting.

6 Using the embroidery needle and yellow perlé embroidery thread, work a line of chain stitch around the edge of the face, stitching close to the fringe.

To make the lion

1 Photocopy the template at 250 per cent onto a piece of paper and cut it out. Using the fabric marker, draw around the outer edge of the face onto the yellow chenille for the front of the beanbag and press under a 1 cm (½ in) hem all around. Trim the template down to the inner line of the face, draw around it onto the brown felt and cut out the back of the beanbag.

2 Cut the eyes and nose out of the template. Iron fusible webbing (see page 8) onto the back of the scrap of brown felt. Use the pencil to draw around the nose and eyes onto the paper backing and cut out. Following the template, iron them in position on the yellow chenille. Using the embroidery needle and three strands of brown embroidery thread, work a line of chain stitch (see page 13) around the nose. With two strands, work chain stitch around each eye.

3 Using three strands of brown embroidery thread, embroider a mouth in chain stitch and French knots (see page 14) for whiskers. Using six strands of black, embroider French knots for pupils.

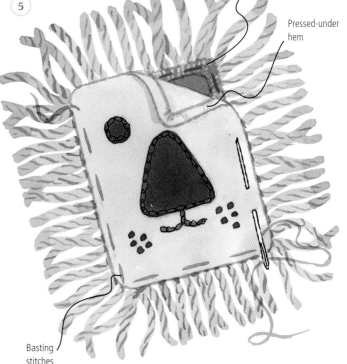

Fringe basted to brown felt

Pressed-under hem

Basting stitches

⑤

To make the pirate

1 Photocopy the template at 250 per cent onto a piece of paper and cut it out. Using the fabric marker, draw around the edge of the template onto both pieces of brown felt and cut out the shapes. Set one piece aside.

2 Cut the bandanna out of the template. Draw around it onto the red felt and cut out the shape. Cut six 1 cm (½ in) diameter circles from white felt. Using a tiny dab of fabric glue and following the template, stick the circles to the red felt and leave to dry. Using white sewing thread and stab stitch (see page 15), sew around the edges of each circle.

3 Apply a few dabs of glue to the back of the red felt and stick it in position on one of the brown pieces. Leave to dry. Using the hand-sewing needle and red sewing thread, work stab stitch across the curved lower edge of the bandanna.

4 Cut the eye patch, moustache and eye out of the template. Iron the fusible webbing (see page 8) onto the back of the scraps of black and green felt. Using the pencil, draw around and then cut out a black eye patch, moustache and eye pupil and a green eye. Peel off the paper backings and iron the elements in position on the face. Using matching sewing threads and stab stitch, sew around the edges of each shape.

5 Using the embroidery needle and two strands of black embroidery thread, work French knots (see page 14) for nostrils. Using six strands, work the strap for the eye patch in chain stitch (see page 13).

Getting it right
To give a beanbag the right degree of floppiness, don't completely fill it with lentils. About half full should be just right.

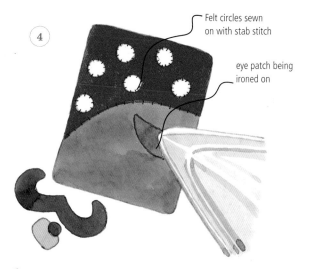

④

Felt circles sewn on with stab stitch

eye patch being ironed on

6 Wrong sides facing, pin the face to the brown felt piece set aside in Step 1. Using the hand-sewing needle and blanket stitch (see page 13), sew the two pieces together around the edges. Use brown sewing thread for the face section and red sewing thread for the bandanna section. Before completing the sewing, half-fill the beanbag with dried lentils.

7 To make the earring, loop a length of yellow embroidery thread twice around your forefinger and knot the ends. Using two strands of yellow embroidery thread, work blanket stitch (see page 13) over the looped threads right around the circle, stitching over the knot. Stitch the earring to the edge of the beanbag at the bottom left corner of the bandanna.

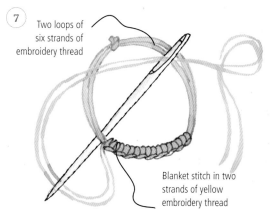

⑦ Two loops of six strands of embroidery thread

Blanket stitch in two strands of yellow embroidery thread

To make the dog

1 Photocopy the template at 250 per cent onto a piece of paper and cut it out. Using the fabric marker, draw around the outer edge of the face onto both larger pieces of pale-brown needlecord, with the ridges on the fabric running lengthways. Cut out both pieces and set one aside.

2 Iron the fusible webbing (see page 8) onto the back of the 7 x 8.5 cm (2¾ x 3¼ in) piece of dark-brown needlecord. Cut the eye patch piece out of the template and, using the pencil, draw around it onto the paper backing, ensuring that the ridges run at right angles to the main face piece. Cut out the eye patch. Peel the paper backing off the webbing and, following the template, iron it into position on one of the face pieces. Using the hand-sewing needle and dark-brown sewing thread, work blanket stitch (see page 13) around the curved edge.

3 Cut the outer eyes and the nose out of the template. Iron fusible webbing onto the backs of the scraps of white and black felt and cut out two white eyes and one black nose. Peel off the paper backings and iron the features into position on the face. Using matching sewing threads, work blanket stitch around them. Using two strands of black embroidery thread, sew the buttons onto the whites of the eyes.

4 Cut the tongue from the template and use this to cut a red felt tongue. Using matching sewing thread, work blanket stitch around the curved edges. Oversew the straight edge of the tongue in place just below the nose.

5 Using the embroidery needle and two strands of black embroidery thread and following the template, embroider a mouth in chain stitch (see page 13). Make sure the chain stitch runs over the top of the stitched-down end of the tongue.

6 Draw around the ear template onto both pieces of pale-brown cotton and both remaining pieces of needlecord. Right sides facing, pin the needlecord pieces to the cotton pieces in pairs. Thread the sewing machine with pale-brown thread and set it to a medium straight stitch. Taking a 1 cm (½ in) seam allowance, machine-sew around the curved edges, leaving the short straight edge open. Trim and clip the seams (see page 12), turn the ears right side out and press.

Button being sewn on for eye

7 Following the ear placement marks on the template, lay the ears right-side up, at a slant, on the face, placing the dark-brown ear on the side with the eye patch. Baste the ears in position. Lay the needlecord piece set aside in Step 1 right-side down on the face. Machine-sew around the edges, taking a 1 cm (½ in) seam allowance and leaving a 4 cm (1½ in) gap in the bottom edge for turning and filling.

8 Turn the beanbag right side out and press the side seams, pressing under the edges of the gap. Fill the beanbag with dried lentils and ladder stitch (see page 11) the gap closed.

Making a difference

You can make both the dog and lion beanbags entirely in felt if you prefer. For the lion, simply cut a piece of yellow felt the same size as the brown felt to make the lion's face. For the dog, leave off all the seam allowances and join the front and back with blanket stitch in the same way as for the pirate. Make the ears from a single layer of felt edged with blanket stitch and catch them into the edge stitching in the appropriate places.

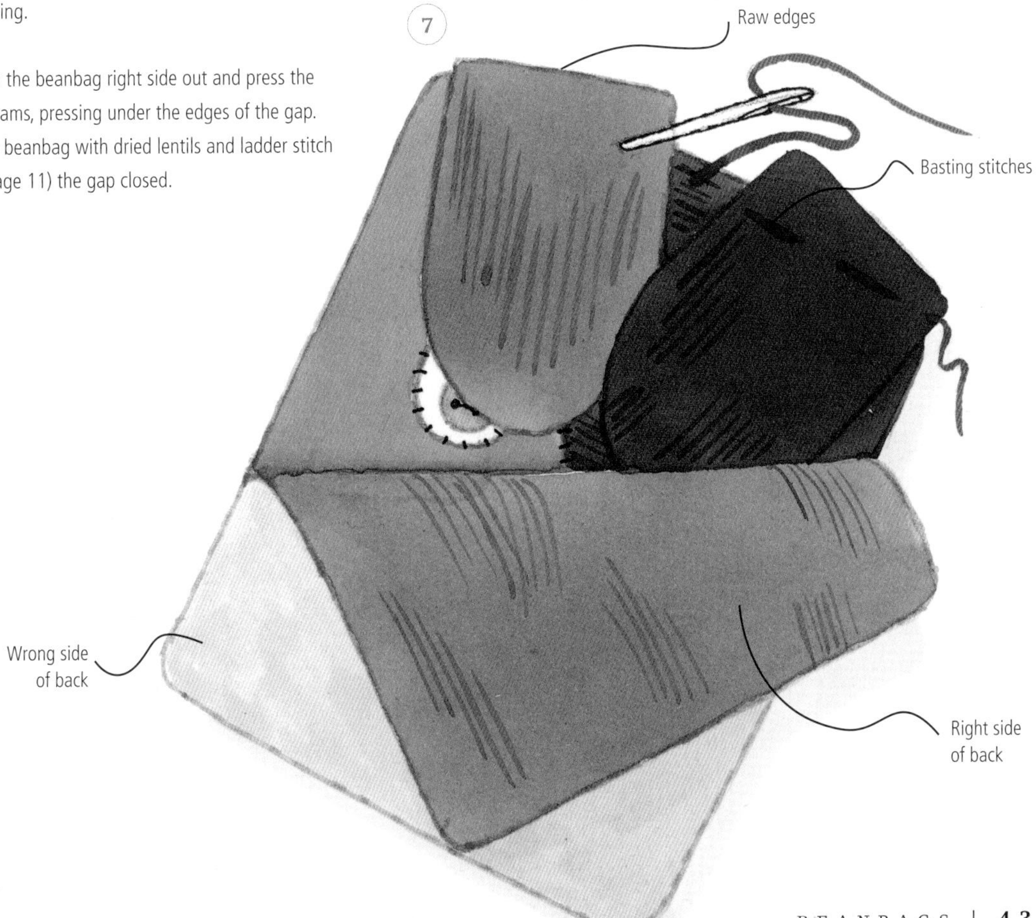

7

Raw edges

Basting stitches

Wrong side of back

Right side of back

THREE MICE

Cute and colourful, these little mice are simple and speedy to sew. Make the embroidered curls as intricate as you wish, or leave them off completely. Create a family of them in an evening and perch them around the playroom.

MATERIALS

For each mouse:

Paper for template

Three 10 x 6.5 cm (4 x 2½ in) and two 3-cm (1¼-in) square pieces of felt

Black sewing thread

Two circular and one flat oval black beads

Stranded embroidery thread in two colours

Toy stuffing

EQUIPMENT

Mouse template, page 118

Paper scissors

Fading fabric marker

Fabric scissors

Hand-sewing needle

Embroidery needle

Pins

TECHNIQUES

Embroidery techniques, pages 13–16

Stuffing a toy, page 19

1 Photocopy the template at 120 per cent onto a piece of paper and cut it out. Using the fabric marker, draw around the body onto each of the larger pieces of felt and cut out the three shapes. Set one shape aside.

2 Using the hand-sewing needle and black sewing thread, follow the template to sew a circular bead onto each remaining shape to make eyes.

3 Using the embroidery needle and two strands of one colour of embroidery thread, embroider chain-stitch swirls (see page 13) onto the two felt pieces. Embroider freehand or, if you prefer, mark the swirls first with the fabric marker. Remember that you need to work on the opposite sides of the two pieces to create the left- and right-hand sides of the body.

4 Cut the ear out of the template. Draw around it onto the two smaller pieces of felt and cut out two shapes. Using the first colour of embroidery thread, and following the photograph, embroider three straight stitches (see page 15) on each ear. Remember to create a left- and a right-hand ear, as for the body pieces.

6 Wrong sides facing, pin the body pieces together. Starting at the nose, sew the two pieces together along the top edge using blanket stitch and the second colour of embroidery thread.

7 Pin the piece set aside in Step 1 to the two free curved edges of the body. Again, starting at the nose and using blanket stitch, sew the pieces together along one edge.

8 Twist or plait a length of the first colour of embroidery thread to make a tail approximately 10 cm (4 in) long. Tie a large knot in one end. Slip the knot into the body at the tail end and catch it nto the stitching as you blanket stitch the last seam. Before completing the seam, stuff the mouse lightly with toy stuffing.

9 Using the hand-sewing needle and black sewing thread, sew the oval bead to the nose of the mouse.

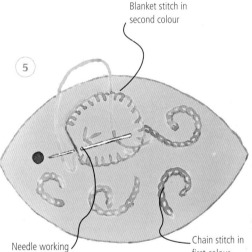

Blanket stitch in second colour

Needle working blanket stitch

Chain stitch in first colour

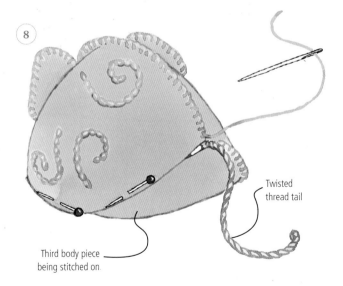

Twisted thread tail

Third body piece being stitched on

5 Using the second colour of embroidery thread and starting at the top of the straight section of the ear, work blanket stitch (see page 13) around the curved edge; do not finish the thread when you reach the end of the curve. Following the template, pin the ear in position then continue the blanket stitch across the straight section of the ear, sewing it to the body piece. Secure the thread on the back. Attach both ears to a body piece.

POCKET DOLL

Tuck trinkets and little treasures into this obliging doll's pocket to keep them safe and sound. A hanging loop allows your child to carry her like a handbag, or hang her up in the playroom.

MATERIALS
Paper for templates
25 x 21 cm (10 x 8¼ in) pieces of pale-brown and printed cotton fabric
Scraps of cream, blue and red fabric
Sewing threads in cream, blue, red, black, pale-brown and colour to match printed cotton
25 x 16 cm (10 x 6¼ in) piece of printed cotton fabric
13 cm (5 in) of 3 mm (⅛ in) cord elastic
Basting thread
14 x 4 cm (5½ x 1½ in) piece of printed cotton fabric
Toy stuffing
Cotton yarn for hair
Scrap of flower trimming

EQUIPMENT
Pocket doll templates, page 118
Paper scissors
Fading fabric marker
Fabric scissors
Iron
Fusible webbing
Pencil
Hand-sewing needle
Sewing machine
Pins

TECHNIQUES
Using fusible webbing, page 8
Hand-sewing techniques, pages 10–12
Finishing a seam, page 12
Embroidery techniques, pages 13–16
Creating a face, page 16
Making hair, pages 17–18
Stuffing a toy, page 19

1 Photocopy the templates at 345 per cent onto a piece of paper and cut them out. Using the fabric marker, draw around the outer edge of the body onto the pale-brown and 25 x 21 cm (10 x 8¼ in) piece of printed cotton. Cut out the shapes and set the printed cotton one aside.

2 Cut the eyes and mouth out of the template. Iron the fusible webbing (see page 8) onto the backs of the scraps of fabric. Using the pencil, draw around the features onto the paper backing and cut out two complete eyes in cream and a mouth in red. Cut the irises out of the eye templates and cut them out in blue.

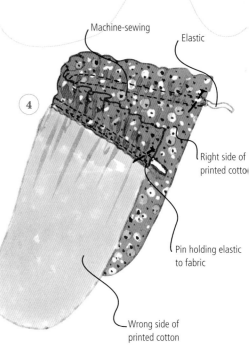

Machine-sewing

Elastic

④

Right side of
printed cotton

Pin holding elastic
to fabric

Wrong side of
printed cotton

4 Draw around the pocket template onto the
25 x 16 cm (10 x 6¼ in) piece of printed cotton. Press
under a 5 mm (¼ in) hem along the long straight (top)
edge, then press under a 1.5 cm (⅝ in) hem. Set the
sewing machine to a medium straight stitch and thread
it with thread that matches the printed fabric. Machine-
sew two lines across the top of the pocket; one line very
close to the lower pressed edge and one line 1 cm (½
in) down from the upper pressed edge. Thread the elastic through the channel between the sewn lines. Gather
the fabric up along the elastic so that about 1 cm (½ in)
of elastic protrudes at each end of the channel and pin
to hold the ends in place.

5 Right sides up, lay the pocket on the pale-brown
body, aligning the lower raw edges. Pin the sides of
the pocket to the sides of the body, matching the raw
edges. Baste along all the raw edges, making sure you
baste through the ends of the elastic. Remove the pins.

3 Peel off the paper backings from the blue irises and
iron them onto the cream eyes. Peel off the rest of the
paper backings and arrange the features on the pale-
brown body, following the template for position, and
iron them in place. Using the hand-sewing needle and
matching sewing threads, work blanket stitch (see page
13) around the features. Using black thread and stab
stitch (see page 15), work tiny stars for the pupils.

8 Machine-sew around the doll, taking a 1 cm (½ in) seam allowance and sewing through all layers. Start at the top and reverse over the ends of the strip to hold them securely. Stop sewing at about the position of the ear (if the doll had one) before the start of the sewing. Turn right side out and press the seam only, pressing under the seam allowances of the gap. Stuff lightly and ladder stitch (see page 11) the gap closed.

9 Using the cotton yarn, make the doll's hair. Create a centre parting (see page 17), then draw the hair into a bunch on each side of the head and stitch it in place. Cut individual flowers from the trimming and, using the hand-sewing needle and thread, sew one over the base of each bunch. Sew another flower to the front of the pocket.

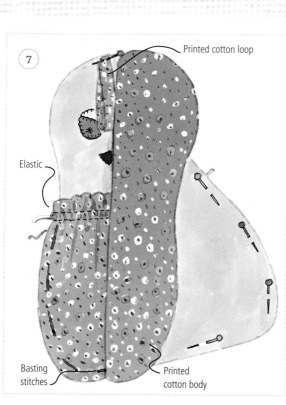

⑦

Printed cotton loop

Elastic

Basting stitches

Printed cotton body

⑨

Printed cotton loop

Yellow cotton yarn

Needle sewing flower to top of hair bunch

Pocket

6 Iron the 14 x 4 cm (5½ x 1½ in) strip of printed cotton in half lengthways. Open it out then press the raw edges to the middle. Fold the strip in half again along the first pressed fold and press again. Machine-sew close to the open long edge. Fold the strip in half widthways and pin the raw ends to the centre top of the head.

7 Right-side down, lay the printed cotton body on top of the pale-brown one and the pocket. Baste around the edges, basting through all layers to ensure that the edges of the pocket and the ends of the strip are all held in position.

CUDDLE UP

PATCHWORK GONK

Soft and squashy, this friendly toy for babies is made from scraps of fabric using a traditional patchwork technique. The preparation of the pentagons may seem time-consuming, but there are only a dozen to make and your gonk will look better if they are properly prepared.

MATERIALS
Paper for templates
Eleven x 10 cm (4 in) squares of
    plain and patterned fabrics
One 15 cm (6 in) square of fabric
Stranded embroidery threads in
    four colours
Scrap of ric-rac trimming
Sewing threads to match fabrics
Basting thread
Scraps of patterned fabrics
Toy stuffing

EQUIPMENT
Gonk templates, page 119
Paper scissors
Fading fabric marker
Fabric scissors
10 cm (4 in) embroidery hoop
Embroidery and
    hand-sewing needles
Pencil
Iron
Knitting needle
Pins

TECHNIQUES
Using an embroidery hoop, page 8
Hand-sewing techniques,
    pages 10–12
Finishing a seam, page 12
Embroidery techniques,
    pages 13–16
Stuffing a toy, page 19

Getting it right

To position printed patterns attractively on a pentagon, you may find it useful to make a reverse template. Draw around the paper template onto a square of thin card. Using a craft knife and ruler and working on a cutting mat, cut out the pentagon shape and discard. Lay the square of card on the fabric so that you can see how the printed pattern appears inside the pentagon and then draw around the inside of the negative shape.

1 Photocopy the templates at 120 per cent onto pieces of paper and cut them out. Using the fabric marker, draw around the outer edge of the pentagon onto each of the eleven 10 cm (4 in) squares of fabric and cut out the shapes. Draw around the template onto the 15 cm (6 in) square of fabric, but do not cut out the shape.

2 Using the fabric marker, draw the gonk's features onto the pentagon on the 15 cm (6 in) square of fabric. Fix the fabric into the embroidery hoop (see page 8). Using the embroidery needle and three strands of thread throughout, embroider the features in chain stitch (see page 13), following the photograph for colours.

3 Using the hand-sewing needle, matching sewing thread and slip stitch (see page 11), sew the ric-rac across the pentagon, just above the eyes. Cut out the pentagon.

4 Trim the template down to the inner dotted line. Using the pencil, draw around this 11 times onto paper and cut out the shapes to make 12 paper pentagons in total. Lay one paper pentagon in the centre of a fabric one. Working around the shape, one edge at a time, fold and press the edges of the fabric over the paper. Using the hand-sewing needle and basting thread, baste the edges of the fabric down, basting through the paper. Make 12 pentagons in this way.

5 Draw around the foot template onto the scraps of fabric and cut out eight shapes. Right sides facing, pin the pieces together in pairs to make four feet. Using the hand-sewing needle, matching sewing thread and backstitch (see page 10), sew the pieces together taking a 5 mm (¼ in) seam allowance. Clip the curves (see page 12), turn right side out and press. You will find a knitting needle useful for turning the feet out.

6 Plan the arrangement of pentagons for the top and bottom sections of the gonk. Lay out one pentagon for the top of the head section and arrange five more around it, one against each straight edge: one of these will be the embroidered face. Make the same arrangement of pentagons for the bottom section, with one pentagon in the centre and five more around it.

7 Follow the illustration to position the feet on the bottom section of the gonk. They should be right side up on the right sides of the pentagons and the raw ends should just overlap the edges of the pentagons. Pin and baste the feet in place, basting both across the base and down the length of each one.

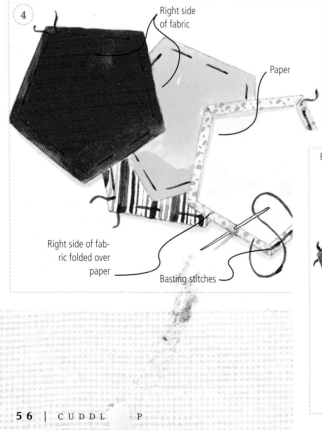

4

Right side of fabric

Paper

Right side of fabric folded over paper

Basting stitches

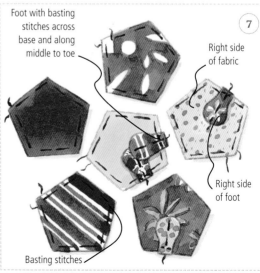

Foot with basting stitches across base and along middle to toe

7

Right side of fabric

Right side of foot

Basting stitches

8 Assemble the top section of the gonk. Right sides facing, pin the centre pentagon to another one along their touching straight edges. Using the hand-sewing needle, matching sewing thread and tiny oversewing stitches (see page 11), sew the pieces together along the edge. Repeat until a pentagon is sewn to each edge of the central one. Now sew the adjoining edges of the pentagons together in the same way to make a cup shape.

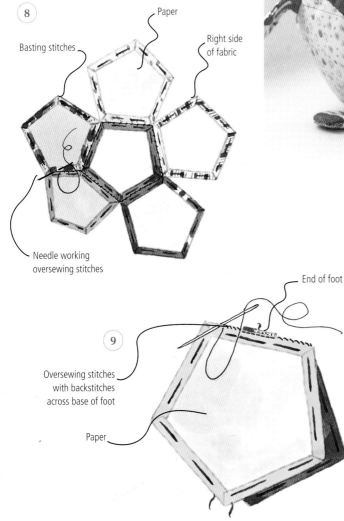

8

Paper

Right side
of fabric

Basting stitches

Needle working
oversewing stitches

9

Oversewing stitches
with backstitches
across base of foot

Paper

End of foot

9 Assemble the bottom section in the same way. When you get to the place where the end of a foot protrudes, change to backstitch (see page 10) to sew across it, sewing very close to the edges of the pentagons and making sure you catch all layers in the stitching.

10 Fit the two halves of the gonk together, wrong sides facing, with the points of one section fitting into the valleys of the other. The upper feet need to be either side of the face and the lower feet below the face. Sew the edges together as in Step 8, but leave two edges open. Stitch across the base of the protruding feet as in Step 9.

11 Remove all the basting and paper templates. Turn the gonk right side out through the opening. Stuff the gonk lightly and ladder stitch (see page 11) the open seams closed.

COOL CAT

An elegant and glamorous cat that little girls will love. There's a handy tip for working perfect lazy-daisy flowers, so this is a great project for novice embroiderers.

MATERIALS

Paper for template
Two 26 x 16 cm (11 x 6¼ in) pieces of cream suedette fabric
Scrap of pink suedette fabric
Pink and blue sewing threads
Small amount of blue novelty eyelash yarn
Pale lilac seed beads
Cream beading thread
Pink, blue and lilac stranded embroidery threads
5 mm (¼ in) translucent purple sequins
Toy stuffing
Scraps of lilac and pink ribbon

EQUIPMENT

Cool cat template, page 119
Paper scissors
Fading fabric marker
Fabric scissors
Iron
Fusible webbing
Pencil
Hand-sewing needle
Cocktail stick
Fabric glue
Beading needle
Embroidery needle
Pins

TECHNIQUES

Using fusible webbing, page 8
Hand-sewing techniques, pages 10–12
Embroidery techniques, pages 13–16
Stuffing a toy, page 19

1 Photocopy the template at 210 per cent onto a piece of paper and cut it out. Using the fabric marker, draw around the outer edge onto one piece of cream suedette. Flip the template over and draw around it again onto the other piece. Cut out the shapes and set one aside.

2 Cut the heart-shaped nose out of the template. Iron fusible webbing (see page 8) onto the back of the pink suedette. Using the pencil, draw around the nose onto the paper backing and cut it out. Peel off the backing and, following the template, iron the nose in position on the head. Using the hand-sewing needle, pink thread and tiny stab stitches (see page 15), sew around the nose.

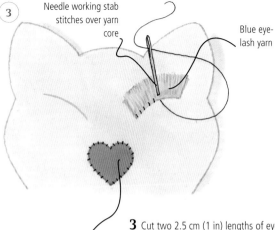

③

Needle working stab stitches over yarn core

Blue eye-lash yarn

Pink suedette edged with stab stitches

over the hole in the middle and then make a small dot at each point of the pentagon. Remove the template. Using the embroidery needle and two strands of embroidery thread, work a lazy daisy (see page 15) over the marks. Bring the needle up through the centre mark and make each petal touch one of the outer marks. Work as many flowers as you wish, using all the colours of thread.

3 Cut two 2.5 cm (1 in) lengths of eyelash yarn. Use the cocktail stick to apply tiny dabs of fabric glue to the woven core of the yarn and stick the strips in position. Using the hand-sewing needle, blue thread and tiny stab stitches, sew over the core of the yarn to hold the strips firmly in place.

4 Using the beading needle and thread, sew on a seed bead at each end of each strip of eyelash yarn. Sew on a few beads either side of the nose.

5 Cut the pentagon shape out of the template: this is the template for stitching the lazy-daisy flowers. Make a hole at the marked centre point with the embroidery needle. Lay the template where you want to work a flower. Press the fabric marker

6 Bring the beading needle and thread up through the middle of a flower. Slip on a sequin and a bead. Skipping the bead, take the needle back down through the sequin only and secure the thread on the back. Repeat on each flower. On each foot work short lines of chain stitch (see page 13) for claws.

7 Wrong sides facing, lay the embroidered cat on top of the plain one. Pin the pieces together close to the edge in just a few places, as pins can mark the fabric. Using the beading needle and thread and starting at the neck and working across the back, sew the two pieces together using beaded blanket stitch. This stitch is worked in the same way as conventional blanket stitch (see page 13), but pick up a bead on each stitch. As you loop the thread under the needle, ensure that the bead slides down to sit next to the previous stitch so that it lies on the edge of the suedette. Make the stitches small and close together to make a continuous beaded edging around the cat.

Getting it right

The flowers for this cat are slim and star-like, but you could use three strands of thread to make the flowers chunkier if you prefer.

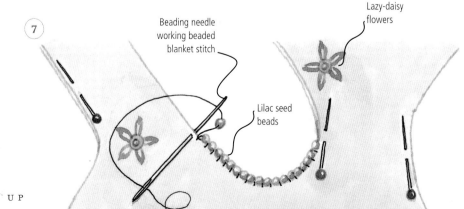

⑦

Beading needle working beaded blanket stitch

Lazy-daisy flowers

Lilac seed beads

8 Firmly stuff the tail as you sew down the outside edge of it. Continue down the back leg and stuff the leg as you sew the inside of it. Stuff the front leg and body as you work back up to the neck. Stuff the head before completing the stitching.

9 Cut 10 cm (4 in) of pink ribbon and fold it into a bow shape with the ends overlapping a little at centre back. Using the hand-sewing needle and pink thread, sew a line of running stitches (see page 10) down the centre, catching both ends in the stitching. Pull the stitches up tightly and secure the thread. Wrap a scrap of lilac ribbon over the gathers and sew the ends together on the back to make a fake bow. Wrap lilac ribbon around the cat's neck and sew the ends together on the front. Sew the bow to the front of the ribbon around the neck, covering the join.

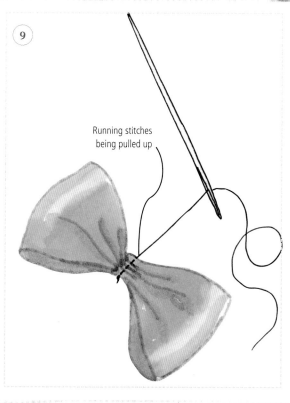

9

Running stitches being pulled up

QUILTED SNAIL

A huge, squashy toy that doubles as a groovy cushion, this snail uses two basic quilting techniques, both great for novices to the craft. The shell is hand-quilted using a quick embroidery stitch and the nose is trapunto quilted.

MATERIALS
Paper for templates
Two 50 x 40 cm (20 x 16 in) pieces of printed cotton fabric
Two 50 x 40 cm (20 x 16 in) and two 45 x 25 cm (18 x 10 in) pieces of plain cotton fabric
Two 50 x 40 cm (20 x 16 in) pieces of polyester wadding
Basting thread
Perlé embroidery thread in dark colour to coordinate with printed cotton
Sewing threads to match fabrics
Two 45 x 25 cm (18 x 10 in) and two 17 x 5 cm (6¾ x 2 in) pieces of contrast printed cotton fabric
One 45 x 25 cm (18 x 10 in) and two 16 x 3 cm (6¼ x 1¼ in) pieces of iron-on shirt canvas
Stranded embroidery threads in two colours to coordinate with contrast printed cotton fabric
Toy stuffing
Beading thread
Small seed beads
Two large and two small buttons

EQUIPMENT
Snail templates, page 120
Paper scissors
Fading fabric marker
Pins
Hand-sewing, embroidery, blunt-tipped embroidery and beading needles
Sewing machine
Fabric scissors
Small, sharp scissors

TECHNIQUES
Hand-sewing techniques, pages 10–12
Finishing a seam, page 12
Embroidery techniques, pages 13–16
Stuffing a toy, page 19

1 Photocopy the templates at 500 per cent onto a piece of paper and cut them out. Using the fabric marker, draw around the outer edge of the shell template onto the right side of both pieces of printed cotton, remembering to flip the template to produce left- and right-hand pieces. Cut around the spiral of the shell template and lay it over the already-drawn outline. Draw around the spiral onto the fabric by running the fabric marker along the cut edges of the paper.

2 Right side down, lay a large piece of plain cotton flat on the work surface then lay a piece of wadding on top of it. Right side up, lay the printed cotton on top of the wadding. Pin the layers together. Using the hand-sewing needle and basting thread, baste around the outer edges of the shell then in a cross shape across it to stop the layers shifting while you quilt.

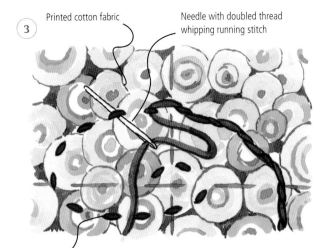

Printed cotton fabric

Needle with doubled thread
whipping running stitch

Running stitch
in perlé thread

3 Using the embroidery needle and perlé thread, work running stitch (see page 10) along the spiral; make the stitches about 1 cm (½ in) long and 1 cm (½ in) apart. Secure the thread on the back. Measure off a length of perlé thread the length of the spiral plus 10 cm (4 in) and double this length. Thread the blunt-tipped embroidery needle and knot the ends together. Using the doubled thread, whip the running stitches (see page 15). Remove the basting stitches.

4 Set the sewing machine to a medium zigzag stitch and sew around the outer edge of the shell, just outside the drawn line. Trim off excess fabric and wadding close to the line of zigzag stitching. Make up the second shell piece in the same way.

Getting it right

The technique used for the snail's nose is called 'trapunto' quilting, and it is worked on two layers of fabric without any wadding between them, as described in Step 6. The result is flat fabric with a raised, stuffed shape on the front.

5 Using the fabric marker, draw around the outer edge of the body template onto the right side of both pieces of contrast printed cotton, remembering to flip the template after drawing around it the first time to produce left- and right-hand pieces. Lay a body piece right side up on each of the remaining, right side down, pieces of plain cotton. Set the sewing machine to a medium zigzag stitch and sew around the outer edge of the body, just outside the drawn line. Iron the large piece of shirt canvas onto the plain cotton backing of one body piece. On both pieces, trim off excess fabric close to the line of zigzag stitching.

6 Using the fading fabric marker, draw the nose and mouth onto the piece of cotton without the stiffening. Using the embroidery needle and three strands of stranded embroidery thread, work a line of chain stitch (see page 13) around the nose. Turn the piece over and pinch just the plain cotton within the circle of chain stitch. Using the small, sharp scissors, make a little snip in the plain cotton, being very careful not to cut the printed cotton. Push toy stuffing (see page 19) through the hole to fill the embroidered circle. Using the hand-sewing needle and sewing thread, oversew (see page 11) the cut in the plain cotton closed.

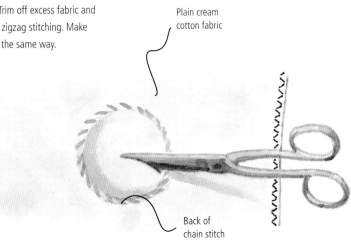

6

Plain cream
cotton fabric

Back of
chain stitch

7 Right sides facing, pin and then baste the body pieces to the shell pieces. You are matching an outward curved edge to an inward curved edge, so accurate basting is needed to make sure the seams lie flat and smooth. Set the sewing machine to a medium straight stitch and carefully machine-sew the seams. Remove the basting.

8 Right sides facing, pin and baste the two snail pieces together around the outside edges, leaving a 20 cm (8 in) gap in the bottom edge. Machine-sew around the edges. Turn the snail right side out through the gap.

9 Place the two small strips of shirt canvas on the two small strips of contrast printed cotton, aligning the raw edges at one short end and having an equal overlap around the other three sides. Iron the canvas in position. Fold the excess fabric over the edges of the canvas and press. Fold each piece in half lengthways and machine-sew the long edges together, stitching very close to the edge, to make narrow tubes. Reshape the tubes so that the seams lie centre back.

10 On each tube, using the beading needle and thread and small oversewing stitches, sew the short edge with the fabric overlap closed, picking up a bead with every stitch.

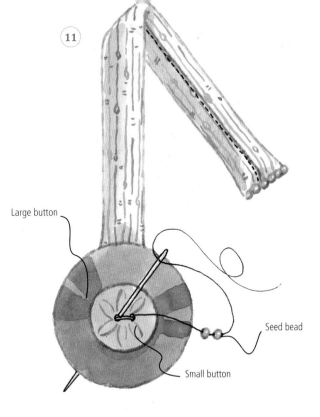

(11)

Large button

Seed bead

Small button

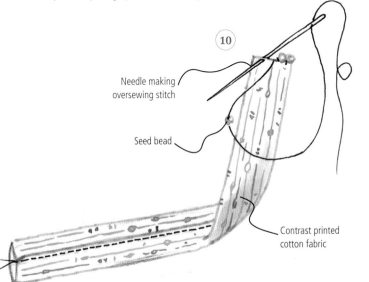

(10)

Needle making
oversewing stitch

Seed bead

Contrast printed
cotton fabric

11 Using the hand-sewing needle and thread, sew the remaining open edge of each tube to the back of a large button. Then sew a smaller button into the middle of the large button, threading on two seed beads as you make the last stitch through both buttons.

12 Sew both buttons and tubes to the head as eyes and antennae. Sew through the holes in the buttons and slip stitch (see page 11) around the base of the stalk to hold them in position.

13 Stuff the whole snail with toy stuffing through the gap in the bottom of the shell. Ladder stitch (see page 11) the gap closed.

INDIAN ELEPHANT

This is a good project for novice embroiderers: there isn't a lot to do, the stitches are simple, and if you make a mistake you can unpick the stitches and the felt won't show the marks.

MATERIALS
Paper for templates
Two 20 x 13 cm (8 x 5 in),
    two 5 x 4 cm (2 x 1½ in) and
    two 7 x 11 cm (2¾ x 4½ in)
    pieces of grey felt
Selection of stranded
    embroidery threads
Two 7 x 11 cm (2¾ x 4½ in) pieces
    of medium-weight iron-on
    interfacing
Grey sewing thread
Toy stuffing

EQUIPMENT
Elephant templates, page 120
Paper scissors
Fading fabric marker
Fabric scissors
Embroidery and
    hand-sewing needles
Pins
Iron

TECHNIQUES
Hand-sewing techniques,
    pages 10–12
Embroidery techniques,
    pages 13–16
Stuffing a toy, page 19

1 Photocopy the templates at 140 per cent onto a piece of paper and cut them out. Using the fabric marker, draw around the body onto the two largest pieces of felt and draw around the ears onto the two 5 x 4 cm (2 x 1½ in) pieces of grey felt. Cut out all of the shapes.

2 Using the embroidery needle and two strands of embroidery thread, work blanket stitch (see page 13) around the curved edge of the ear. Start at the top of the straight section and do not finish the thread when you reach the end of the curve. Pin the ear in position on the head following the placement mark on the body template and continue the blanket stitch across the straight section of the ear, sewing it to the body piece (see Step 5 of Three Mice, page 47). Secure the thread on the back. Repeat with the second ear, making sure you flip the body piece so that you have both a left- and right-hand side of the elephant.

4 Cut along the dotted line on the template to cut out the leg gusset. Iron iron-on interfacing following the manufacturer's instructions onto the two remaining pieces of felt. Draw around the gusset onto the felt, remembering to flip the template over after drawing around it the first time to make left- and right-hand pieces. Right sides facing, pin the gusset pieces together along the straight edge and, using the hand-sewing needle and grey sewing thread, oversew (see page 11) them together.

5 Wrong sides facing, pin the embroidered body pieces together. Using the embroidery needle, three strands of embroidery thread and starting in the crook of the neck, work blanket stitch along the underside of the trunk. Continue along the top of the trunk, stuffing it as you go (see page 19).

3 Using the photograph as a guide, embroider the elephant's body pieces. You can make both sides the same, or different as here. Use three strands of embroidery thread throughout. Blanket stitch and chain stitch (see page 13) work well for outlining the blanket on the elephant's back. Fill in the blanket with lazy-daisy flowers (see page 15) linked with lines of backstitch (see page 10). Use French knots (see page 14) for the flower centres. Embroider a flower on the elephant's forehead and one or two on the trunk. Work lines of chain stitch down the trunk and legs, with individual lazy daisy stitches for toes. Use a circle of chain stitch with a French knot in the middle to make the eyes.

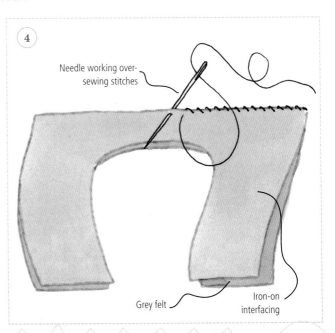

④

Needle working over-sewing stitches

Grey felt

Iron-on interfacing

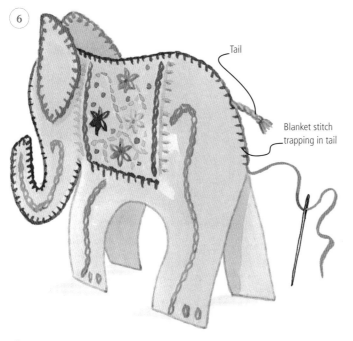

Tail

Blanket stitch trapping in tail

7 Wrong sides facing, pin the gusset into position between the legs of the embroidered body pieces. Match the front and back legs on the bodies and gusset. Continue the blanket stitch down one back leg. Stitch across the foot and up the other side of the leg, stuffing it as you go. Stitch across the tummy, down the front leg and up the other side, again stuffing the leg as you go. When you reach the crook of the neck, secure the thread.

8 Go back to the tail and continue the blanket stitch to attach the other side of the gusset to the second embroidered body. Sew and stuff in the same way, but stuff the body and head as well. Finish the stitching in the crook of the neck.

6 Stitch over the back of the elephant to the tail point marked on the template. Plait or coil a short length of embroidery thread and knot both ends. Trim one end to make a short tassel. Slip the other end into the body of the elephant and continue the blanket stitch, securing the tail in place. Stitch to the point where the gusset starts, as shown on the template, but do not cut the thread.

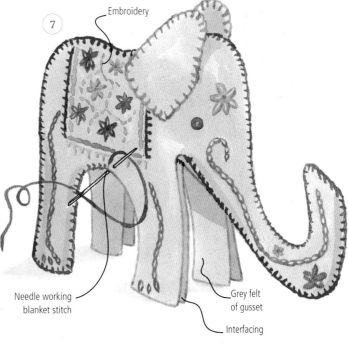

Embroidery

Needle working blanket stitch

Grey felt of gusset

Interfacing

INDIAN ELEPHANT | **69**

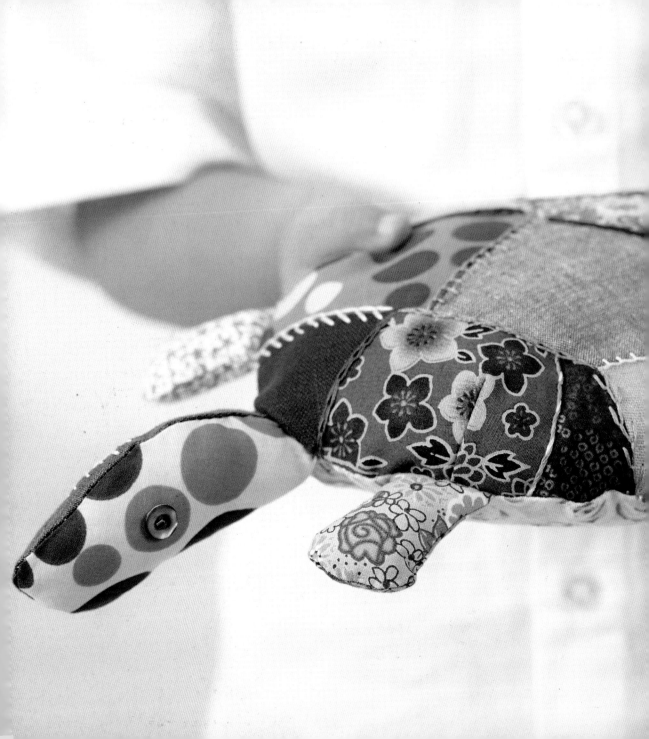

CRAZY TORTOISE

Raid your scrap bag for fabrics to make this crazy patchwork tortoise and let your creative flair run riot with embroidery stitches to embellish him.

MATERIALS

Paper for templates
20 x 17 cm (8 x 6¾ in) piece
    of fabric
Scraps of plain and
    patterned fabrics
Basting and sewing threads
Stranded embroidery threads
Toy stuffing
Beading thread
Two small two-hole buttons
Two small black hex beads

EQUIPMENT

Tortoise templates, page 121
Paper scissors
Fading fabric marker
Fabric scissors
Pins
Hand-sewing, embroidery and
    beading needles
Sewing machine
Iron

TECHNIQUES

Hand-sewing techniques,
    pages 10–12
Finishing a seam, page 12

Embroidery techniques, pages
    13–16
Stuffing a toy, page 19

1 Photocopy the templates at 250 per cent onto a piece of paper and cut them out. Using the fabric marker, draw around the outer edge of the shell onto the large piece of fabric. Cut out the shape and set it aside.

2 Cut along the solid marked lines on the shell template. Pin each piece to a scrap of fabric and cut around the template piece, adding a 1 cm (½ in) seam allowance all around. Fold the edges of the fabric over the template piece and baste them in place. One at a time, pin the shapes together right sides facing, following the original template. Using tiny stitches, oversew (see page 11) the pieces together on the wrong side. Remove the basting and the paper template pieces.

Choosing fabrics

Select printed fabrics with a small pattern and plain fabrics that pick up the colours in the printed designs. Keeping to a limited colour palette will prevent the tortoise from being too crazy.

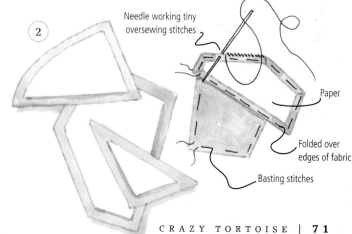

2

Needle working tiny
oversewing stitches

Paper

Folded over
edges of fabric

Basting stitches

Getting it right

The easiest way to transfer the darts is to make small holes in the relevant template pieces at the tip of the darts. Lay the template piece over the appropriate fabric piece and press the fabric marker against the hole in the template. A dot will appear in the right place on the fabric. Using the marker, make small dots on the fabric at the wide ends of the dart on the template. Remove the template and fold the fabric so that the two wide-end dots meet and the fold finishes at the marked inner point. Pin or baste the dart in place.

5 Wrong sides facing, fold scraps of fabric in half. Draw around the leg and tail templates onto the fabrics. Flip the leg templates over and draw around them again so that you have left- and right-hand sets of both legs. Cut out the shapes and pin pairs of pieces together with right sides facing. Using the hand-sewing needle, matching sewing thread and backstitch (see page 10), and taking a 5 mm (¼ in) seam allowance, sew around the legs and tail, leaving the short straight ends open. Turn right side out and press. Stuff lightly then baste across the open ends.

3 Transfer the dart markings from the template to the shell. Thread the sewing machine with matching thread and set it to a small straight stitch. Starting at the edge of the shell, machine-sew the darts.

4 On the right side, embroider over the seams in the patchwork shell. You can use any stitches you want for this, including chain stitch, feather stitch, single-arm feather stitch, blanket stitch with regular and uneven legs and whipped running stitch (see pages 13–15).

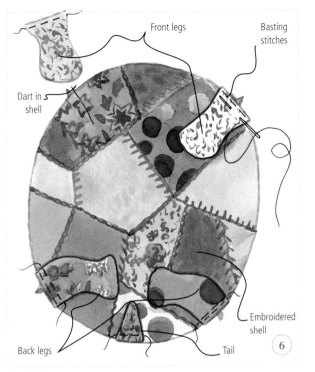

Front legs

Basting stitches

Dart in shell

Back legs

Tail

Embroidered shell

6

8 Make up the head in the same way as the legs and tail, following Step 5 but using two different fabrics. When basting across the open end, fold the neck in half so that the seams meet before basting across it. Using the beading needle and thread, sew on buttons and beads for eyes, coming up through one hole in the button, slipping the bead onto the needle and then going down through the other hole.

9 Slip the neck into the opening at the front of the shell. Slip stitch (see page 11) across the underside of the neck, sewing the lower shell to the underside of the neck, then slip stitch across the top, sewing the embroidered upper shell to the top of the neck.

6 Right sides facing, lay the legs on the shell with the open ends over the ends of the darts and in alignment with the raw edges of the shell. Follow the illustration to position them so that they are the right way around when the body is turned out. Baste in place across the ends of the legs. Position the tail centrally between the two back legs and baste in place.

7 Right sides facing, lay the shell piece set aside in Step 1 on the top of the embroidered shell. Baste around the edges, leaving a 4 cm (1½ in) gap centrally between the two front legs. Machine-sew around the shell, taking a 1 cm (½ in) seam allowance. Set the sewing machine to a zigzag stitch and sew around the shell just outside the first line of stitching. Remove the basting, trim excess fabric, clip the curves (see page 12) and turn right side out. Stuff the body lightly through the gap.

9

Head seam

Needle working slip stitch

Button eye with bead pupil

Front leg

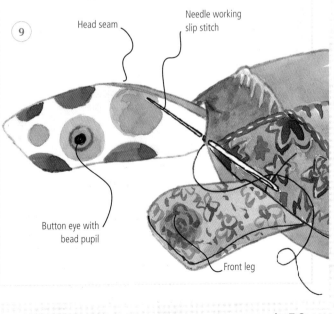

FELT BEAR

A traditional bear with an upturned nose and a fat tummy, this lovable bruin has jointed arms and legs attached with buttons. Here he is stitched with thread that matches the felt, but you could use a contrast colour if you prefer.

MATERIALS

Paper for templates
Two 25 x 13 cm (10 x 5 in),
    one 15 x 5 cm (6 x 2 in),
    eight 15 x 6 cm (6 x 2½ in),
    two 4 x 3 cm (1½ x 1¼ in) and
    two 5 x 4 cm (2 x 1½ in) pieces
    of felt
Sewing thread to match felt
Toy stuffing
Stranded embroidery thread in
    darker shade of felt colour
Two small four-hole buttons and
    four large two-hole buttons
DK-weight knitting yarn in
    any colour

EQUIPMENT

Bear templates, page 121
Paper scissors
Fading fabric marker
Fabric scissors
Pins
Hand-sewing, embroidery and long
    darner or doll needles
Knitting needles the size
    recommended on the yarn
    ball band

TECHNIQUES

Embroidery techniques, pages
    13–16
Stuffing a toy, page 19

1 Photocopy the templates at 290 per cent onto pieces of paper and cut them out. Using the fabric marker, draw around the outer edge of the body onto both large pieces of felt. Draw around the head gusset onto the 15 x 5 cm (6 x 2 in) piece of felt. Draw around the arms four times and the legs four times onto 15 x 6 cm (6 x 2½ in) pieces. Draw around the ears onto both 4 x 3 cm (1½ x 1¼ in) pieces and the foot onto both 5 x 4 cm (2 x 1½ in) pieces of felt. Cut out all the shapes.

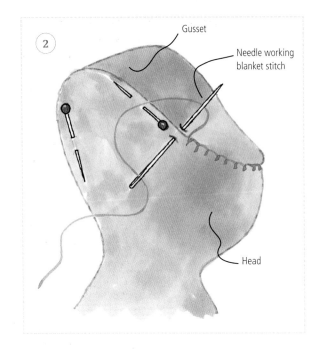

Gusset

Needle working blanket stitch

Head

5 Using the embroidery needle and three strands of embroidery thread, follow the photograph to work a line of chain stitch (see page 13) for the mouth. Work straight stitches (see page 15) across the tip of the snout to make the nose.

6 Thread the long darner needle or doll needle with a long length of three strands of embroidery thread and knot the end. At the position of the eyes, take the needle straight through the head, pulling the thread all the way through. Thread on a small button and take the needle back through the diagonally opposite hole in the button. Take the needle back through the head to appear next to the knot. Thread on another button in the same way. Go back through to the first button and pull the thread tight to indent the eyes a little. Repeat the stitches through the holes in the buttons, but going through the free ones to make cross-stitches. Go through the head and buttons twice more then secure the thread by knotting it around itself under one of the buttons.

2 Starting at the tip of the snout, pin the gusset to one side of the head. Using the hand-sewing needle, matching sewing thread and blanket stitch (see page 13), sew the gusset to the head piece. Pin the other side of the gusset to the other head piece and sew them together in the same way.

3 Starting at the bottom of the curved edge of an ear, work blanket stitch around the curve; do not finish the thread when you reach the end of the curve. Following the photograph, pin the ear in position then continue the blanket stitch across the back of the straight section of the ear, sewing it to the body piece. Secure the thread on the back (see Step 5 of Three Mice, page 47).

4 Below the gusset, pin the two body pieces together and continue the blanket stitch right around the body. Before completing the stitching, stuff the head and body firmly (see page 19).

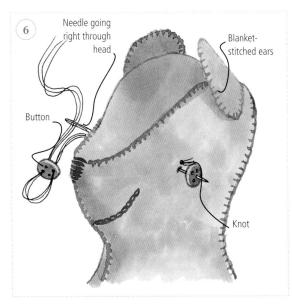

Needle going right through head

Blanket-stitched ears

Button

Knot

7 Pin two arm pieces together. Using the hand-sewing needle and sewing thread, work blanket stitch around the edge. Before completing the stitching, stuff the arm firmly. Repeat with the remaining pair of arm pieces.

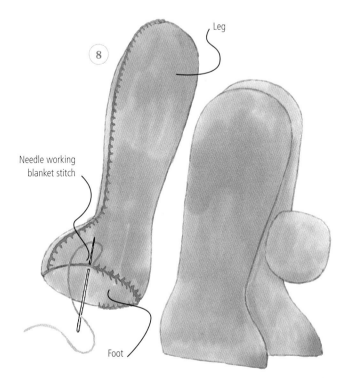

Leg

Needle working blanket stitch

Foot

9 Attach the arms and legs in a similar way to the eyes. Thread the long darner needle or doll needle with a long length of six strands of embroidery thread and knot the end. Take the needle through the top of one arm then through the body at the point marked on the template, then through the top of the other arm. Thread on a large button and take the needle back through the other hole in the button. Go back through the body very close to where you first came through and through the first arm. Thread on a second button in the same way as the first one. Go back and forth through the arms, body and buttons several times then secure the thread by knotting it around itself under one of the buttons. Attach the legs in the same way as the arms.

10 To knit a scarf, cast on eight stitches and knit every row until the scarf is the desired length. Cast off. Make a fringe by cutting short lengths of yarn and looping them through the cast on and cast off ends, knotting them securely. Alternatively, fray the edges of a strip of printed cotton fabric and use that as a scarf for the bear.

8 Pin two leg pieces together. Starting at the toes work blanket stitch up the leg and down the other side. Stuff the top section of the leg firmly. Fit the foot into the base of the leg and work blanket stitch around it. Before completing the stitching, stuff the rest of the leg firmly. Repeat with the remaining pair of leg pieces.

RAG DOLL

As she doesn't have separate clothes, this doll is quite straightforward to make. From the tips of her dainty boots to the top of her curly head, she's a classic rag doll.

MATERIALS
Paper for templates
Two 12 cm (4¾ in) squares, two
    15 x 9 cm (6 x 3½ in) pieces and
    one 60 x 22 cm (24 x 8⅓ in)
    piece of striped cotton fabric
Two 22 x 12 cm (8¾ x 4¾ in)
    pieces of plain red cotton fabric
Scraps of brown and cream fabric
Two 12 cm (4¾ in) squares of
    cream cotton fabric
Dark-brown, apple-green and two
    shades of pink stranded
    embroidery threads
Sewing threads to match all fabrics
Toy stuffing
Basting thread
1 m (1 yd) of ric-rac
Tiny button
Two seed beads
30 x 25 cm (12 x 10 in) piece of
    brown cotton fabric

EQUIPMENT
Rag doll templates, page 122
Paper scissors
Fading fabric marker
Fabric scissors
10 cm (4 in) embroidery hoop
Embroidery needle
Pins
Sewing machine
Iron
Knitting needle
Hand-sewing needle

TECHNIQUES
Using an embroidery hoop, page 8
Hand-sewing techniques,
    pages 10–12
Finishing a seam, page 12
Embroidery techniques, pages
    13–16
Creating a face, page 16
Making hair, page 17–18
Stuffing a toy, page 19

1 Photocopy the templates at 290 per cent onto pieces of paper and cut them out. Using the fabric marker, draw around the outer edge of the torso onto both 12 cm (4¾ in) squares of striped fabric. Draw around the arms onto both 15 x 9 cm (6 x 3½ in) pieces of striped fabric and the legs onto both pieces of plain red fabric. Draw around the boots four times onto scraps of brown fabric and the hands twice onto scraps of cream fabric. Cut out all the shapes. Draw around the head onto both squares of cream cotton fabric, but cut out only one shape.

2 Fit the uncut head piece into the embroidery hoop (see page 8) and embroider the face. Using the embroidery needle, two strands of dark-brown thread and tiny chain stitch (see page 13) and starting in the inner corner, embroider the upper eyelid. Using one strand of dark-brown, embroider the lower lid with backstitch (see page 10), stopping before you meet the inner corner of the eye. The eyelashes are also lines of dark-brown backstitch. Using tiny chain stitch and two strands of apple-green thread, embroider concentric circles for the irises of each eye. Work dark-brown French knots (see page 14) for the pupils and nostrils. Work chain-stitch for the mouth with two strands of pink thread. Outline the lips with the darker shade and fill them in with concentric lines in the lighter shade. When the embroidery is complete, cut out the head.

3 Right sides facing, pin a boot to the base of each leg, making sure you pin them on to make left- and right-hand feet. Set the sewing machine to a small straight stitch and thread it with red thread. Taking a 1 cm (½ in) seam allowance, machine-sew the seams. Press the seam allowances towards the boots.

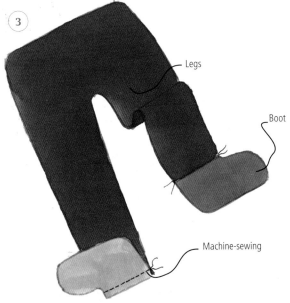

Legs

Boot

Machine-sewing

4 Right sides facing, pin the pieced boot and leg sections together, aligning the boot seams. Starting at the top on one side of the legs and taking a 1 cm (½ in) seam allowance, machine-sew around the legs and boots, leaving the top open. Turn right sides out, and press. Press under a 1 cm (½ in) seam allowance around the top of the legs. Using the embroidery needle and two strands of dark-brown thread, embroider a line of chain stitch around the tops of the boots, over the seams joining them to the legs.

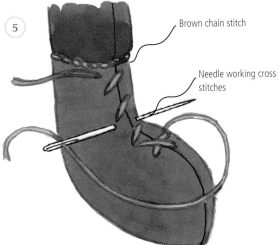

Brown chain stitch

Needle working cross stitches

5 Stuff the boots firmly, using the knitting needle to push the stuffing down into them. Stuff the legs lightly. Thread the embroidery needle with a long length of three strands of dark-brown thread. Make a stitch through the front of a boot and pull the thread halfway through. With the threaded end, make diagonal stitches up the front of the boot. Thread the needle with the other end of the thread and work diagonal stitches in the opposite direction up the front of the boot to make crossed laces. Tie the ends of the threads in a bow.

6 Right sides facing, pin the body pieces together and follow the template to machine-sew both shoulder seams: on each side, start at the outer edge and sew to the neck placement mark, reversing a few stitches at the end of the line of stitching to secure the threads. Press the seam allowances open, pressing under the allowances across the neck gap at the same time.

7 Right sides facing, pin the hands to the ends of the arms. Taking a 1 cm (½ in) seam allowance, machine-sew the seams. Press the seam allowances open. On the right side, lay a piece of ric-rac over the seam and sew it in place. Fold the tops of the arms in half lengthways and make a crease with your fingers.

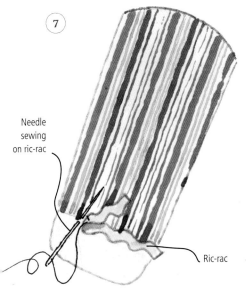

⑦

Needle
sewing
on ric-rac

Ric-rac

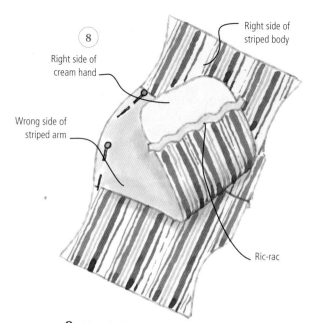

Right side of
striped body

Right side of
cream hand

Wrong side of
striped arm

Ric-rac

8 Right sides facing, pin the tops of the arms to the body. Align the creases in the tops of the arms with the shoulder seams and ease the curves around the tops of the arms to lie flat along the body pieces. Taking a 1 cm (½ in) seam allowance, machine-sew the seams. Press the seam allowances towards the body.

9 Right sides facing, fold the body section in half along the shoulder seams, folding the arms in half lengthways. Make sure the ends of the ric-rac around the wrists align. Starting at the folded edge of one hand and taking a 1 cm (½ in) seam allowance, sew around the hand, along the underarm and down to the bottom of the body. Repeat on the other side of the body. Turn right side out but do not press. Stuff the arms lightly, using the knitting needle to push stuffing down them.

10 Slip 1 cm (½ in) of the bottom of the body section into the top of the legs and pin the pieces together. Using the hand-sewing needle and matching thread, slip stitch (see page 11) the body to the legs. Stuff the body lightly through the gap at the neck.

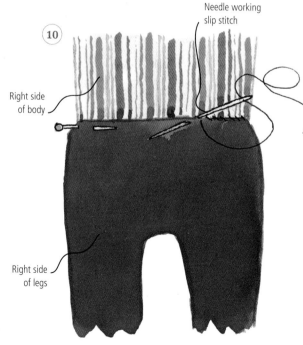

Needle working
slip stitch

(10)

Right side
of body

Right side
of legs

11 Thread the sewing machine with cream thread. Right sides facing and taking a 1 cm (½ in) seam allowance, machine-sew around the head, leaving the bottom of the neck open. Turn right side out but do not press. Stuff the head through the neck. Slip 1 cm (½ in) of the neck into the gap in the top of the body. Pin and slip stitch the sections together, as in Step 10.

12 Press under a 1 cm (½ in) double hem along one long edge of the large piece of striped fabric. On the right side, pin and then baste a length of ric-rac to the fabric, 3 mm (⅛ in) up from the pressed edge. Thread the sewing machine with thread to match the ric-rac. Machine-sew in a straight line along the middle of the ric-rac, sewing the hem at the same time. Press under a single 1 cm (½ in) hem on the other long edge.

13 Right sides facing, fold the fabric in half widthways, aligning the hemmed edges. Machine-sew the short edge. Press the seam allowances open. Using the hand-sewing needle and matching thread, work a line of running stitches (see page 10) along the pressed fold of the single hem. Slip the doll's legs into the skirt and pull up the running stitches to gather the top of the skirt to fit around the doll's waist. Secure the thread firmly. Slip stitch the skirt in position around the waist.

14 Sew a length of ric-rac around the doll's waist to cover the stitching at the top of the skirt. Sew another length around the neck to cover the seam between the body and neck. Sew the button to the centre front of the ric-rac around the neck, slipping two seed beads onto the thread as you sew it on (see Step 11 of the Quilted Snail, page 65).

15 Cut the 30 x 25 cm (12 x 10 in) piece of brown fabric into lengthways strips. Fray the edges of each strip by pulling out a few threads. Use these strips to make hair in a similar way to yarn. Sew strips along the top of the head first to make a fringe, allowing about 2 cm (¾ in) to lie across the forehead. Use a backstitch (see page 10) to hold each strip in position. Sew more strips down the centre of the head to make a centre parting. To curl the hair, twirl each strip around once or twice before sewing it down at ear level.

15

Rag strips with frayed edges

Ric-rac

Button and bead broach

CUTE
CREATIONS

PUFF CLOWN

Bright colours lend a fresh twist to a classic toy. Made from Suffolk puffs, or yo-yos as they are called in the US, this clown has stretchy arms and legs. Though there are quite a few steps, he's really very simple to make.

MATERIALS
59 x 14-cm (5½-in) diameter
    circles of cotton fabric
Sewing threads to match fabrics
    and felts
Paper for templates
Scraps of black, orange, red, pale-
    blue and bright-pink felt
90 cm (35 in) of black elastic cord
Five 1-cm (½-in) diameter and one
    2-cm (1-in) two-hole buttons and
    one 2-cm (1-in) four-hole button
Toy stuffing
Four small pom-poms
Scrap of cream cotton fabric
Two tiny black buttons
Scraps of ric-rac and fake-fur trim

EQUIPMENT
Hand-sewing needle
Puff clown templates, page 122
Paper scissors
Fading fabric marker
Fabric scissors
Pins
Large-eyed embroidery needle
Iron
Fusible webbing
Pencil
Sewing machine

TECHNIQUES
Using fusible webbing, page 8
Hand-sewing techniques,
    pages 10–12
Embroidery techniques, pages 13–16
Stuffing a toy, page 19

1 Make 57 of the cotton circles into Suffolk puffs. Using matching thread, sew a line of small running stitches (see page 10) around the edge of each circle, turning under a narrow hem as you go. Pull the stitches up as tightly as possible and secure the puff with a few tiny oversewing stitches (see page 11) on the gathered edge. Flatten the puff with your fingers so that the gathered hole is in the centre.

Choosing fabrics
This toy is perfect for using up scraps of fabric from your stash and from recycled clothes. This example uses seven brightly coloured plain fabrics, but you can use any colour combinations or patterned fabrics. When you are threading up the legs, arms and body, thread the colours on in a different order for each element.

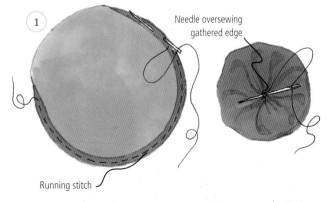

Needle oversewing
gathered edge

Running stitch

2 Photocopy the templates at 180 per cent onto a piece of paper and cut them out. Using the fabric marker, draw around the shoe template onto black felt and cut out four shoes. Pin the shoes together in pairs. Using the hand-sewing needle, black sewing thread and blanket stitch (see page 13), sew the pairs together around the edges. Start at the top of the heel, then work across the sole. Stop sewing halfway along the top of the foot, but do not secure the thread.

3 Cut two 30 cm (12 in) lengths of elastic. Thread one end of each piece through a hole in a small button and firmly knot it over the edge of the button. Make a few stitches through the knot to make sure it won't come undone. Stuff the shoes firmly. Slip a button into each foot so that the elastic comes out at the top of the heel and complete the blanket stitching, trapping the button securely into the shoe. Sew a pom-pom to the toe of each shoe.

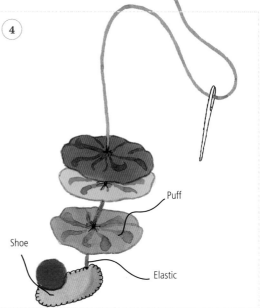

4

Puff

Shoe

Elastic

4 Thread the free end of one length of elastic into the large-eyed needle. Take the needle through the centre of the back of a puff and through the gathered hole on the other side. Thread on 14 puffs in this way and repeat with the other length of elastic. Push the puffs down to the shoes.

5 Thread the ends of the elastic through the holes in the larger two-hole button and slide the button down to sit on top of the puffs. Tie the ends of the elastic together in a double knot on top of the button, but do not cut the elastic. Do not stretch the elastic before you knot it.

Getting it right

You can make your own pom-poms in the traditional way using yarn and two cardboard circles, or, as here, cut pom-poms from a strip of furnishing trimming. Most shops will happily sell you a tiny amount of trimming and if you unpick it you can use the thread holding the pom-pom to the trimming band to sew the pom-poms on with.

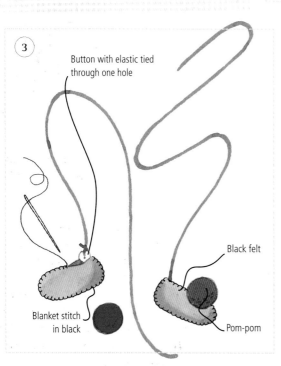

3

Button with elastic tied through one hole

Black felt

Blanket stitch in black

Pom-pom

6 Work running stitch around the edge of one of the remaining cotton circles as in Step 1, but do not pull it up. Thread both ends of the elastic through the middle of the circle and push it down to sit on top of the button. Now pull up the gathering stitches tightly so that the puff encloses the button. Secure the thread as in Step 1. (If you interleave the top two or three puffs on each leg, the legs will sit neatly side by side.)

(6)

Button with elastic through holes and knotted

7 Thread both ends of the elastic through eight more puffs as in Step 4, taking the needle through the back of the fabric first so that the gathered hole is uppermost.

8 Using the fabric marker, draw around the glove template onto orange felt and cut out four gloves. Cut two 15 cm (6 in) lengths of elastic and knot them onto two small buttons as in Step 3. Follow Steps 3 and 4 to make up the arms in the same way as the legs, trapping the buttons in the blanket-stitched and stuffed gloves and threading nine puffs onto each arm. However, this time take the elastic through the gathered hole in each puff first, then through the fabric on the back. Do not sew pom-poms onto the gloves.

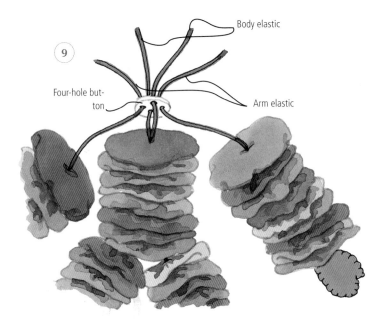

Body elastic

Four-hole button

Arm elastic

10 Gather the edge of the remaining cotton circle and, as in Step 6, thread it onto the body elastic and pull the gathers up to cover the button. Thread on the remaining three puffs, gathered hole uppermost. Thread the end of the elastic through the remaining small button and slide it down to sit on top of the last puff. Knot the elastic through one button hole and secure it with a few stitches as in Step 3. Trim off any excess elastic.

11 Iron fusible webbing (see page 8) onto scraps of red and pale-blue felt. Using the fabric marker, draw around the head template onto cream cotton and cut out two heads. Cut the mouth, nose and eyes out of the template. Using the pencil, draw around them onto the paper backings and cut out a nose and mouth in red felt and two eyes in pale-blue felt. Peel the backings off the webbing and, following the template, iron the features into position on one of the head pieces. Using matching sewing thread and tiny stab stitches (see page 15), stitch around each feature. Using black sewing thread, sew on the tiny buttons for the pupils of the clown's eyes.

9 Thread the ends of elastic coming out of the body through two diagonally opposite holes in the four-hole button. Thread the arm elastics through the remaining two holes. Pull all the elastics through the button until the arms sit squarely either side of the body and the button is as close to the top of the body as possible without pulling the arms in too tight. Knot the body elastics together with a secure double knot and then knot the arm elastics together, making sure the arms are the same length. As with the legs, do not stretch the elastics before knotting them. Make a few stitches through the knots to secure them and cut off excess arm elastic and one end of body elastic.

12 Right sides facing, pin the two head pieces together. Set the sewing machine to a small straight stitch. Starting at the chin, machine-sew the head pieces together, stopping 2 cm (¾ in) before you get back to the chin. Turn right side out and stuff the head (see page 19). Slip the chin over the button on top of the body and slip stitch the gap closed to attach the head. Before you secure the thread, make a few reinforcing stitches through the cotton fabric on either side of the elastic 'neck'.

13 Using the fabric marker, draw around the whole hat template onto orange felt and cut two hat pieces. Cut the hatband off the hat template. Draw around it onto pink felt and cut two hatbands. Using matching sewing thread and blanket stitch, sew the hat pieces together. Again using matching thread, use blanket stitch to sew the short edges of the hatband together. Then sew the hatband to the hat, oversewing (see page 11) the top edge of the band to the hat about 5 mm (¼ in) up from the lower edge of the hat.

14 Cut a length of fake fur trim, 2 cm (¾ in) longer than the bottom edge of one side of the hat. Starting just in front of one of the side seams of the hat, sew the top edge of the fake fur trim to the lower edge of the orange part of the hat, so that the hatband hides the stitching. Stop sewing just in front of the other side seam and trim off any excess fur so that the furry hair sits symmetrically in the hat.

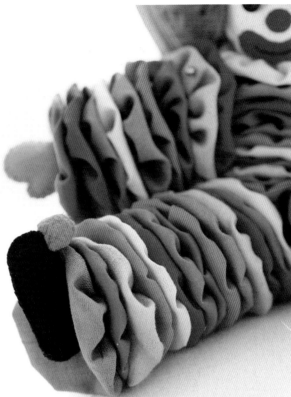

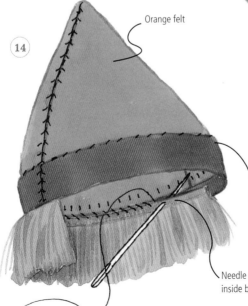

14

Orange felt

15 Slip stitch (see page 11) the hat to the head, positioning it at a jaunty angle. When stitching through the furry hair, be careful not to get the hair caught up in the stitches. Slip stitch a length of ric-rac around the bottom edge of the hatband. Sew a pom-pom to the top of the hat and another to the centre front.

Pink felt hatband

Needle oversewing band of fur to inside bottom edge of orange felt

RABBIT PJ CASE

Straightforward to make, this sleepy rabbit will tidy away pyjamas or a
nightdress and will snooze happily on your child's pillow all day. Make it
in fabric to coordinate with the bed linen for extra style.

MATERIALS
Paper for templates
One 28 cm (11 in) square of each
   of plain cotton, printed cotton
   and medium-weight iron-on
   interfacing
Scraps of white, green and
   brown felt
Brown, green and white stranded
   embroidery threads
50 cm (20 in) of 12 mm (½ in)
   bias binding
Sewing threads to match fabrics
One 16 x 9 cm (6¼ x 3½ in) piece
   of each of plain cotton, printed
   cotton, medium-weight iron-on
   interfacing and heavy-weight
   sew-in interfacing
Basting thread
80 x 4 cm (32 x 1½ in) strip of
   printed cotton

EQUIPMENT
Rabbit templates, page 123
Paper scissors
Fading fabric marker
Fabric scissors
Fusible webbing
Iron
Pencil
Embroidery and hand-sewing
   needles
Pins
Sewing machine

TECHNIQUES
Using fusible webbing, page 8
Hand-sewing techniques,
   pages 10–12
Embroidery techniques, pages
   13–16
Finishing a seam, page 12

1 Photocopy the templates at 290 per cent onto a piece of paper and
cut them out. Using the fabric marker, draw around the outer edge of
the circular face onto the large pieces of plain and printed cottons and the
large piece of interfacing. Cut out the shapes and set the printed cotton
and interfacing aside.

2 Cut the eyes, nose and teeth out of the template. Iron fusible webbing
(see page 8) onto the backs of the scraps of felt. Using the pencil, draw
around the whole eye twice onto the paper backing of the white felt and
cut the eyes out. Cut the eye iris out of the template and draw around it
twice onto green felt and cut these out. Cut the eye pupils out of the
template and draw around them twice onto brown felt and cut them
out. Cut out the teeth in white and the nose in brown felt.

3 Peel the paper backings off the pupils and, following the template, iron them into position on the green irises. Peel the backings off the irises. Using the embroidery needle and three strands of brown embroidery thread, work blanket stitch (see page 13) around the pupils, securing the thread on the back. Iron the irises onto the whites of the eyes then peel the paper backings off the whites. Using three strands of green embroidery thread, work blanket stitch across the curved upper part of the iris to attach it to the whites; do not secure the thread. Iron the whites in position on the circle of plain cotton and continue the blanket stitch around the rest of the irises, attaching them to the cotton. Work blanket stitch around the whites of the eyes with three strands of white embroidery thread.

4 Iron the nose and teeth into position on the cotton and work blanket stitch around them using three strands of matching embroidery thread. Backstitch (see page 10) the line dividing the two teeth with three strands of white embroidery thread. Using three strands of brown embroidery thread and chain stitch (see page 13), embroider the mouth and whiskers onto the cotton.

5 Following the manufacturer's instructions, iron the iron-on interfacing onto the back of the embroidered cotton. This stiffens it and prevents the backs of the stitches catching when pyjamas are pushed into the case.

6 Mark the ear placements on both the printed and plain cotton circles. Pin a length of bias binding over the edge of the section of circle between the inner ear placement marks. Set the sewing machine to a medium zigzag stitch and sew along the binding, sewing both sides to the cotton at the same time.

7 Draw around the ear template twice onto the smaller pieces of plain and printed cotton and both types of interfacing: remember to flip the template over after drawing around it once to create left- and right-hand ears. Cut out the shapes. Iron the iron-on interfacing onto the backs of the plain cotton ears. Lay the printed cotton ears face down on the plain cotton ears and lay the sew-in interfacing on the top. Baste around the edges through all layers. Set the sewing machine to a medium straight stitch and, taking a 1 cm (½ in) seam allowance, machine-sew around the curved edges, leaving the short, bottom edge open. Trim the seam allowances and clip the curves (see page 12). Turn right side out and press.

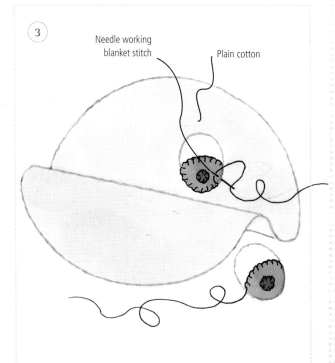

③

Needle working
blanket stitch

Plain cotton

8 Lay the ears plain side down on the plain cotton face, positioning them according to the ear placement marks and aligning the raw edges. Baste in place. Lay the printed cotton circle face down on top, ensuring that the bias-bound section lies between the ears. Pin the layers together. Taking a 1 cm (½ in) seam allowance, machine-sew around the circle, starting and stopping 1.5 cm (⅝ in) inside the inner edge of the ears. Set the sewing machine to a medium zigzag stitch and sew around again, just outside the first line of stitching. Trim excess fabric, clip the curves, turn right side out and press, pressing under the bias-bound 1 cm (½ in) seam allowance on the open section between the ears.

9 Press the long strip of printed cotton in half length-ways. Open it out and, one at a time, press the long raw edges to the centre fold. Press under 1 cm (½ in) at each short end. Fold the strip back in half along the centre fold and press again. Set the sewing machine to a medium straight stitch and, using matching thread, machine-sew along the long, open edge, very close to the folds. Cut the strip in half across the width.

10 Positioning it centrally, tuck the cut end of one half of the strip under one pressed-under seam allowance between the ears. Fold it back up so that it sticks straight up between the ears and pin in place. Repeat with the other strip on the other seam allowance, making sure the strips are placed in the same position on both pieces. One at a time, machine-sew along the open edges, 5 mm (¼ in) in from the edge, catching the printed strip in the stitching. Tie the strips in a bow to close the pyjama case.

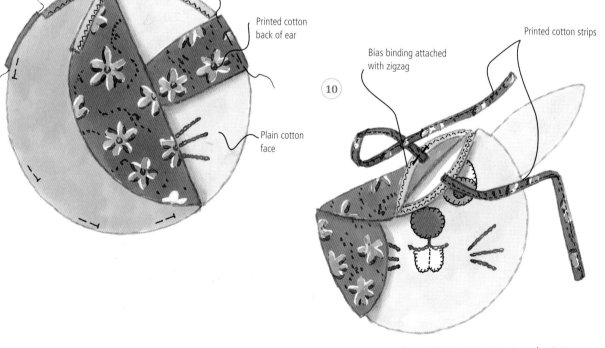

Bias binding attached with zigzag

Printed cotton back of ear

Plain cotton face

Bias binding attached with zigzag

Printed cotton strips

STRIPY SNAKE

This gorgeous snake can be put together easily. You just need to be able to sew straight lines and stitch on buttons and beads. He can be as colourful and decorative as you like and the jingle in his tail adds to his charm.

MATERIALS

Paper for template
85 x 10 cm (33½ x 4 in) piece of brown paper
Two 85 x 10 cm (33 x 4 in) pieces of green cotton fabric
Scraps of ribbons and flat trimmings, from 6 mm (¼ in) to 5 cm (2 in) in width
Basting thread
1 m (1 yd) narrow ric-rac
Sewing thread in colours to match ribbons, green fabric and buttons
Scrap of pink suede or felt
Buttons and beads to embellish
Two 1.5 cm (⅝ in) pearl flat buttons
Two 1 cm (½ in) matt pink sequins
Two pale-blue seed beads
Two pale-pink seed beads
Toy stuffing
Three small bells

EQUIPMENT

Snake template, page 123
Paper scissors
Long ruler
Pencil
Fading fabric marker
Fabric scissors
Pins
Fusible webbing
Iron
Hand-sewing needle
Sewing machine
Beading needle and thread
Knitting needle (optional)

TECHNIQUES

Using fusible webbing, page 8
Hand-sewing techniques, pages 10–12
Finishing a seam, page 12
Embroidery techniques, pages 13–16
Stuffing a toy, page 19

Baby safe

To make the snake a suitable toy for a baby, decorate it with just the ribbon stripes and embroider the snake's eyes and nostrils, rather than sewing on any buttons and beads that might be pulled loose.

1 Photocopy the template at 250 per cent onto a piece of paper and cut out the head and tail. Place the head and tail opposite one another on the brown paper, positioning them so that the nose and tip of the tail are 85 cm (33½ in) apart. Draw around the head and tail and then use the long ruler and pencil to draw lines between the two sections to complete the snake. Cut out the full snake template. Using the fabric marker, draw around the template onto both pieces of green fabric and cut out two snake bodies. Set one body aside.

2 Lay the other snake body right side up and arrange and pin the scraps of ribbon across its width. Each ribbon piece should overlap the edges of the fabric by about 1 cm (½ in) on each side. You need to fuse or baste the ribbons in position before you can machine-sew them. Fusible webbing is best for heavier ribbons, such as satin, velvet or grosgrain. Cut strips narrower than the ribbons and shorter than the width of the snake's body. Iron the strips to the backs of the ribbons, peel off the paper backings and iron the ribbons in position on the fabric. Ensure that each ribbon is at right angles to the edge of the fabric to create neat stripes across the snake.

3 Fusible webbing will show through finer ribbons, such as silk or lightweight polyester, so it is best to baste these in position. Baste along each side of the ribbon, a little way in from the edges. Baste a narrow strip of ribbon from the nose of the snake to the first vertical strip of ribbon.

4 Lay the second snake body right side up, and baste the length of ric-rac in position from nose to tail, arranging it in gentle curves and keeping it at least 1 cm (½ in) in from the edges of the green fabric.

5 Set the sewing machine to a medium straight stitch and, using threads to match the ribbons, machine-sew each piece of ribbon in position, stitching as close as possible to its edges. Sew all the ribbons that require the same colour thread, then change threads and sew another batch. Repeat until all the ribbons are sewn on. Machine-sew the ric-rac in place with a single line of stitching along its middle. Carefully remove all the basting.

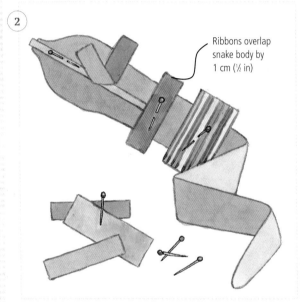

(2)

Ribbons overlap snake body by 1 cm (½ in)

(5)

Machine stitches very close to edge of ribbon

Basting stitches

Getting it right

If you are unsure whether you can use fusible webbing on a specific ribbon (see Step 2), iron a piece onto a leftover scrap of ribbon to see whether it shows through. Ribbons in man-made fibre may crinkle or melt under the heat of the iron so these will need basting rather than fusing (see Step 3).

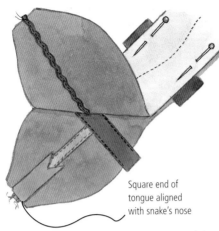

Square end of
tongue aligned
with snake's nose

6 Cut the scrap of pink suede or felt into a slim rectangle with a fork in one end for the snake's tongue. Lay this on top of the snake's head, right sides together, with the square end aligned with the snake's nose.

7 With right sides facing, pin the snake pieces together. Using green thread, machine-sew around the snake, taking a 5 mm (¼ in) seam allowance and leaving a 10 cm (4 in) gap in one side for turning and stuffing. Set the machine to a narrow zigzag stitch and sew around the snake, just outside the stitched line. Trim any excess fabric and ends of ribbon. Turn the snake right side out and press flat, pressing under the seam allowance on the open section.

8 Embellish the snake further by sewing on buttons and beads, placing them to best advantage on the stripes. Using a beading needle and thread, bead the edges of ribbon stripes by whip-stitching (see page 15) the existing line of machine-sewing, picking up a bead before taking the needle under the next machine-stitch.

9 Sew the two pearl buttons in place for the snake's eyes. Coming up through one hole in a button, thread on a pink sequin and blue seed bead then, skipping the bead, take the needle back down through the sequin

and the other hole in the button. Take the needle through the sequin and bead several times in the same way to attach them securely. Sew on two pink seed beads for the snake's nostrils.

10 Now stuff (see page 19) the snake's head and the end of the tail firmly. To stuff the tail, you might find the blunt end of a knitting needle useful for pushing the stuffing down the body. Insert a little stuffing through the gap in the snake's side, then a bell, then more stuffing, the second bell, more stuffing and the third bell. The stuffing between the bells will prevent the tail being lumpy.

11 Stuff the body quite lightly, so that it can bend. When you have finished stuffing the snake, ladder stitch (see page 11) the gap closed.

Button, sequin and seed
bead stitched in place

Beading needle with bead
on thread going back
down through the sequin

OCEAN LINER

Watch your child sail off and explore unknown territories under the dining table with this majestic liner. The basic shapes are simple, while the embroidery can be as detailed as you wish.

MATERIALS
Paper for templates
Two 30 x 8 cm (12 x 3 in) pieces of grey felt
Two 30 x 8 cm (12 x 3 in) and one 20 x 4 cm (8 x 1½ in) pieces of pale-blue felt
Stranded embroidery threads in white, five shades of blue, grey and black
Two 14 x 2.5 cm (5½ x 1 in) pieces of white felt
Scraps of red and black felt
Red, black and white sewing threads
Toy stuffing

EQUIPMENT
Ocean liner templates, page 124
Paper scissors
Fading fabric marker
Fabric scissors
Iron
Fusible webbing
Pencil
Embroidery needle
Hand-sewing needle

TECHNIQUES
Using fusible webbing, page 8
Hand-sewing techniques, pages 10–12
Embroidery techniques, pages 13–16
Stuffing a toy, page 19

1 Photocopy the templates at 250 per cent onto a piece of paper and cut them out. Using the fabric marker, draw around the outer edge of both hull templates onto the grey felt and cut out the shapes.

2 Cut the waves out of the templates. Iron fusible webbing (see page 8) onto the two larger pieces of pale-blue felt. Using the pencil, draw around the waves onto the paper backing of the webbing and cut out the shapes. Peel off the paper backings and, following the templates, iron the waves into position on the hulls, making sure you have a left- and a right-hand hull.

Needle whipping chain stitch with black thread

3 Using the embroidery needle and three strands of thread throughout, embroider the waves and anchor. Embroider short lines of white chain stitch (see page 13) along the crests of the waves. Using one shade of blue, embroider blanket stitch (see page 13) in the troughs of the waves, between the lines of chain stitch. Make the legs of the stitches uneven in length. Using the remaining shades of blue thread and white, work lines of running stitch (see page 10) that echo the curls of the waves. Make the stitches different lengths. Embroider the anchor in grey chain stitch and the flukes in black backstitch (see page 10). Using black thread and stab stitches (see page 15), embroider a star within the circle at the top of the anchor, then whip (see page 15) the chain stitch with black. Whip the black flukes with grey thread.

4 Draw around the superstructure template onto both pieces of white felt. Iron fusible webbing onto the scraps of red and black felt. Cut the funnels out of the template and draw around the large section onto the red felt and the smaller tops onto the black felt. Cut out the shapes, peel off the backings and iron the pieces onto the white superstructures, making sure you flip one of them to create left- and right-hand pieces.

5 Using the hand-sewing needle and matching sewing threads, work lines of tiny running stitch across the top and bottom of the red sections and across the bottom of the black section.

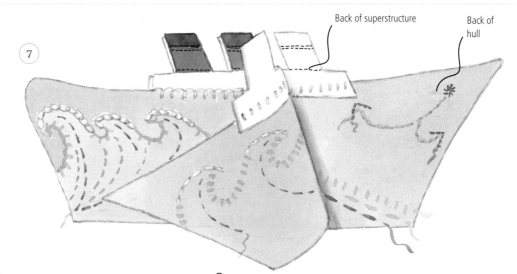

Back of superstructure

Back of hull

7

6 Lay the right side of a superstructure piece against the wrong side of a hull piece, positioning it between the placement marks on the template and with 1 cm (½ in) of superstructure behind the hull. Using the embroidery needle, three strands of grey thread and blanket stitch, sew the two pieces together; make the legs of the blanket stitch of even lengths. Repeat to join the other superstructure piece to the other hull piece.

7 Wrong sides facing, place the two boat pieces together. Using the embroidery needle, three strands of grey thread and blanket stitch, sew the two hull pieces together. Start at the bottom of the bow and sew around to the superstructure then secure the thread. Start again at the bottom of the stern and sew around to the superstructure. Using the hand-sewing needle, sewing threads and blanket stitch, sew the two superstructure pieces together, changing thread colours as appropriate.

8 Draw around the base template onto the remaining piece of pale-blue felt and cut out the shape. Using the embroidery needle, three strands of the first shade of blue thread and uneven blanket stitch, sew the base to one side of the hull. Start at one end and fit the curved edge of the base against the straight edge of the hull.

9 Stuff the liner with toy stuffing (see page 19) through the open edge of the hull. Stuff the funnels firmly and the rest lightly. Sew the other side of the base to the other side of the hull.

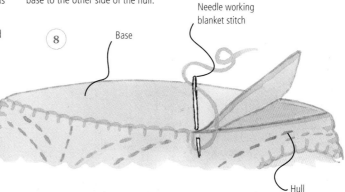

Needle working blanket stitch

8

Base

Hull

CUTE DUCK

Put together and sewn in no time, this little duck has pockets for wings so you can tuck in tiny treasures to keep them safe. Make him in classic yellow or your favourite bright colour.

MATERIALS

Paper for template

Two 16 cm (6¼ in) squares and two 12 x 6 cm (4¾ x 2½ in) pieces of yellow felt

Scrap of white felt

Black, pale-blue, orange and variegated orange-yellow stranded embroidery threads

Black sewing thread

Toy stuffing

EQUIPMENT

Duck template, page 124

Paper scissors

Fading fabric marker

Fabric scissors

Iron

Fusible webbing

Pencil

Embroidery and hand-sewing needles

Pins

TECHNIQUES

Using fusible webbing, page 8

Hand-sewing techniques, pages 10–12

Embroidery techniques, pages 13–16

Stuffing a toy, page 19

Baby safe

If the duck is to be given to a baby, then blanket stitch the wings to the body all around, eliminating the pockets. Felt doesn't wash that well, so you could make the duck from cotton fabric. Embroider wings rather than sewing them on, add 1 cm (½ in) seam allowances and machine-sew the body pieces together, leaving a gap in the base for turning and stuffing. Ladder stitch the gap closed.

1 Photocopy the template at 200 per cent onto a piece of paper and cut it out. Using the fabric marker, draw around the outer edge of the body onto both large squares of yellow felt. Cut the wing out of the template and draw around it onto the remaining two pieces of yellow felt. Cut out the shapes.

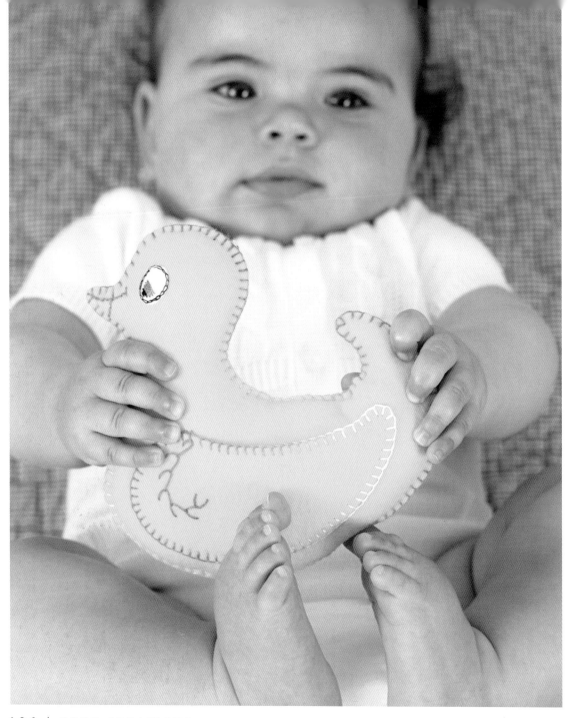

2 Cut the eye out of the template. Iron fusible webbing (see page 8) onto the back of the scrap of white felt. Using the pencil, draw around the eye twice onto the paper backing. Cut out the shapes and peel off the backings. Using the embroidery needle and two strands of thread, work straight stitches (see page 15) in black at the bottom of the eye for the pupil. Using two strands of pale blue, work more straight stitches above the black ones for the irises.

3 Iron the eyes in position on the body pieces, remembering to flip one body piece to create left- and right-hand bodies. Using the hand-sewing needle and black sewing thread, work a line of tiny chain stitches (see page 13) around the outer edge of the eye.

4 Using the embroidery needle, two strands of orange thread and backstitch (see page 10), work lines on both body pieces for the beak. Follow the illustration for position.

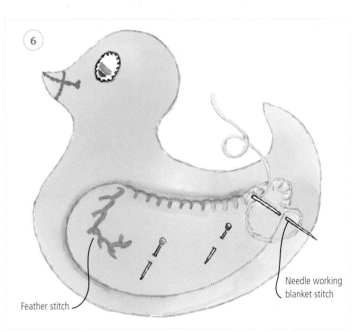

6

Feather stitch

Needle working blanket stitch

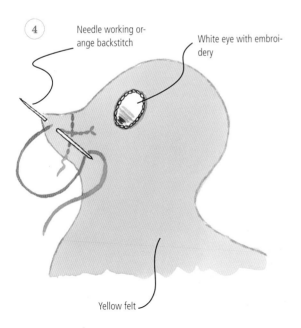

4

Needle working orange backstitch

White eye with embroidery

Yellow felt

5 Using the embroidery needle, three strands of variegated orange-yellow thread and feather stitch (see page 14), embroider a curling line on a wing, starting near the rounded front edge. Work up towards the top edge of the wing then change to blanket stitch (see page 13). Stitch across the top of the wing to about 1 cm (½ in) before the narrow tip of it. Do not cut the thread.

6 Following the template, pin a wing in position on a body piece. Continue the blanket stitches, sewing the wing to the body. When you reach the starting point, take the needle through to the back and secure the thread. Decorate and attach the second wing to the second body piece in the same way.

7 Wrong sides facing, pin the two bodies together. Using the embroidery needle and three strands of variegated orange-yellow thread, work blanket stitch around the edges, joining the two pieces. Before completing the stitching, stuff the toy firmly.

SAUSAGE DOG

Your child will love to play with their very own friendly patchwork pooch. Use scraps of outgrown favourite clothes to make him really special. A sturdier version can sit in front of a draughty window or door in winter.

MATERIALS

Paper for templates
82 x 25 cm (32 x 10 in) piece of lightweight fabric
Scraps of lightweight fabric
Sewing and embroidery threads to match fabrics
Basting thread
Black beading thread
Two 2.5-cm (1-in) diameter buttons with two holes
Two small black beads
Toy stuffing

EQUIPMENT

Sausage dog templates, page 125
Paper scissors
Fading fabric marker
Fabric scissors
Pins
Sewing machine
Iron
Hand-sewing, embroidery and beading needles

TECHNIQUES

Hand-sewing techniques, pages 10–12
Finishing a seam, page 12
Embroidery techniques, pages 13–16
Stuffing a toy, page 19

Choosing fabrics

As a toy for your child, this sausage dog is best made using lightweight fabrics. For a sturdier version, for draughty corners, choose medium-weight furnishing or dress fabrics to give it some substance. (Use lightweight fabrics for the insides of ears and underside of legs to prevent them becoming too bulky.)

1 Photocopy the templates at 455 per cent onto pieces of paper and cut them out. Using the fabric marker, draw around the outer edge of the body onto the large piece of fabric and cut out the shape and set it aside. Cut the body template up along the solid marked lines. Pin each piece to a scrap of fabric and cut it out, adding 1 cm (½ in) seam allowances on all edges other than those on the outer edge of the template, which already include the seam allowance.

2 Cut four ears from the scraps of fabric. Cut two front legs and two back legs from the scraps, then flip the templates and cut two more, so that you have left- and right-hand legs. Set the sewing machine to a small straight stitch and thread it with matching thread. Right sides facing, pin pairs of ears together and machine-sew around the curved edge, taking a 1 cm (½ in) seam allowance and leaving the straight top edge open. Turn right side out and press. Make up the legs in the same way. Set one of each element aside with the complete body piece from Step 1.

3 Make the patchwork side of the sausage dog. Referring back to the template, pin pieces 8 and 10 together, right sides facing, and machine-sew the seam (seam allowances are 1 cm (½ in) throughout). Press the seam allowances open. Pin the seamed section to piece 9, fitting the back leg in position within the seam, as indicated by the placement marks on the template, and sew and press. Join piece 3 to piece 4, fitting the front leg within the seam, then join piece 5 to piece 6. Now pin all the pieces together in the right order and sew all the vertical seams.

4 Press the 1 cm (½ in) seam allowance along the top of an ear to the inside on both edges. Pleat the top of the ear so that the straight edge is the same length as the ear placement mark and baste the pleat in place on the patchwork side of the sausage dog. Make sure that none of the inner ear fabric shows along the top edge. Using the hand-sewing needle and matching sewing thread, slip stitch (see page 11) the ear in position.

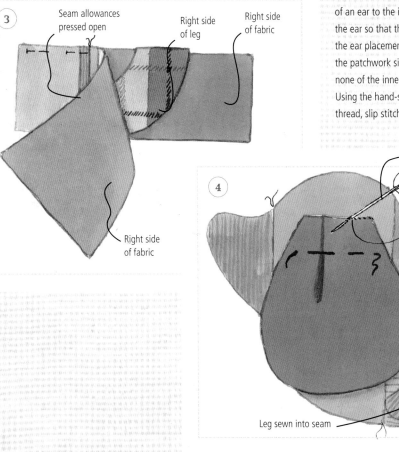

Seam allowances pressed open

Right side of leg

Right side of fabric

Right side of fabric

Needle slip stitching pleated ear

Leg sewn into seam

5 On both edges, press the 1 cm (½ in) seam allowance along the tops of the remaining ear and legs to the inside. Using an embroidery needle, matching embroidery threads and blanket stitch, sew the ears and legs in position on the whole body piece set aside in Step 1.

6 Using the beading needle and thread, sew the buttons to the head as eyes. Bring the needle up through one hole in a button, slip on the bead and take the needle down through the other hole.

7 Roll the ears and feet up and pin them away from the edges of the body on both pieces so that they don't get caught in the stitches. Right sides facing, lay the whole body piece on top of the patchwork body and pin the pieces together, matching the raw edges. Machine-sew around the body, taking a 1 cm (½ in) seam allowance and leaving a 10 cm (4 in) gap in the middle of the underside.

8 Turn right side out and unpin the ears and legs. Stuff the sausage dog with toy stuffing (see page 19) and ladder stitch (see page 11) the gap closed.

Getting it right
When making a sturdier version of this toy, stuff the head and tail lightly with toy stuffing and fill the rest of the body with polystyrene beads, which will give a lovely floppy weight to the dog's body. Pin the gap closed before ladder stitching it.

FLOWER DOLL

This decorative doll is a must for keen embroiderers. Follow the photograph for embellishments or make up your own flower designs using your favourite embroidery stitches and colours of thread.

MATERIALS

Paper for templates
Two 25 cm (10 in) squares and one 8 x 12 cm (3 x 4¾ in) piece of cotton fabric
Scraps of cream linen
Scraps of silk fabric
Two 25 cm (10 in), two 15 cm (6 in) squares and one 8 x 12 cm (3 x 4¾ in) piece of calico
Embroidery threads in colours to tone with cotton fabric
Tiny seed and delica beads in colours to tone with cotton fabric
Beading thread and sewing threads in colours to tone with main fabric
Two 15 cm (6 in) squares of cream linen
Basting thread
Toy stuffing
30 cm (12 in) of 5 mm (¼ in) wide trimming or ribbon
Sewing thread to match trim
Stranded embroidery threads in four shades of yellow-brown

EQUIPMENT

Flower doll templates, page 125
Paper scissors
Water-soluble fabric marker
Iron
Fusible webbing
Pencil
Small, sharp scissors
17 cm (6¾ in) and 10 cm (4 in) embroidery hoops
Hand-sewing, embroidery and beading needles
Fabric scissors
Sewing machine
Knitting needle (optional)

TECHNIQUES

Using fusible webbing, page 8
Using an embroidery hoop, page 8
Hand-sewing techniques, pages 10–12
Finishing a seam, page 12
Embroidery techniques, pages 13–16
Creating a face, page 16
Making hair, page 17–18
Stuffing a toy, page 19

1 Photocopy the templates at 220 per cent onto a piece of paper and cut them out. Lay the doll body template centrally on one of the squares of cotton fabric and draw around it with the fabric marker. Do not cut out the shape.

2 Iron fusible webbing (see page 8) onto the backs of the scraps of cream linen and silk fabric. Cut out the hand templates and, using the pencil, draw around them onto the paper backing on the linen. Draw small flowers onto the paper backing on the silks. Using the small, sharp scissors, cut out all of the shapes. Peel off the backings and position the hands on the dress as shown on the template. Keeping about 5 mm (¼ in) inside the dotted sewing line, arrange the silk flowers on the dress using the main photograph as a guide. Iron all the pieces in place.

5 Draw around the head template onto one of the squares of cream linen. Using the fabric marker, draw the features onto the head. Lay the linen on a 15 cm (6 in) square of calico and, treating the two layers as one fabric, fasten them into the 10 cm (4 in) embroidery hoop (see page 8). Embroider the features. Using the hand-sewing needle and one strand of dark-brown embroidery thread, start the eyes at the top inner corners and embroider the top lid in chain stitch (see page 13) and the bottom lid in backstitch. Using two strands of pale-blue thread, embroider a four-petal lazy daisy in the centre of the eye. Then, using two strands of cornflower-blue, embroider a petal between each of the first four. Make a fake French knot (see page 14) in the middle of each eye. Work French knots (see page 14) in dark-brown thread for the nostrils and use two strands of pink thread to work a mouth in chain-stitch.

6 On the dress and head pieces, baste the layers of fabric together within the seam allowance then cut the pieces out. Following the illustration, and right sides facing, lay the head on the body, matching the raw edges of the bottom of the neck and top of the dress: the dotted line across the neck should match the stitching line at the top of the body

3 Lay the main fabric on one of the 25 cm (10 in) squares of calico. Treating both layers as one, fasten the fabric into the 17 cm (6¾ in) embroidery hoop. Using a hand-sewing needle and one strand of embroidery thread, appliqué the hands and flowers to the dress using small stab stitches (see page 15).

4 Keeping about 5 mm (¼ in) inside the dotted sewing line, embroider flowers, stems and leaves onto the dress, using the main photograph as a guide. You can use whichever embroidery stitches you prefer. You can work some of the embroidered flowers over the appliquéd ones. Use single lazy daisy stitches (see page 15) to make leaves and backstitch and whipped running stitch (see pages 10 and 15) to make stems. Using the beading needle and thread, sew seed or delica beads into the centres of embroidered flowers.

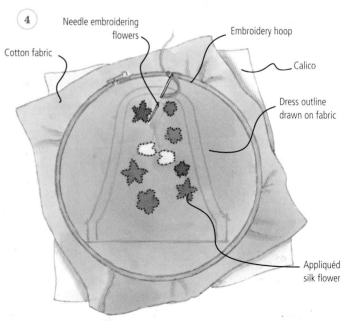

④

Cotton fabric

Needle embroidering flowers

Embroidery hoop

Calico

Dress outline drawn on fabric

Appliquéd silk flower

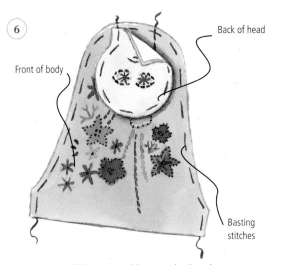

(6)

Back of head

Front of body

Basting stitches

and the neck should be positioned between the dotted placement lines on the body. (Working a line of basting stitches in a contrast thread across these lines will help you position the pieces accurately.) Set the sewing machine to a small straight stitch and, taking a 1 cm (½ in) seam allowance, machine-sew the seam then finger-press the seam allowance open.

7 Make up the back of the doll in the same way as the front, but without the hands, face or flower embroidery. Right sides facing, lay the embroidered front on top of the back, matching the seams at the bottom of the neck. Taking a 1 cm (½ in) seam allowance, machine-sew around the doll, leaving the bottom edge of the body open. Trim the seam allowances and clip the corners (see page 12) and turn right side out. Turning the head out through the narrow neck can be tricky, but careful use of a knitting needle will help. Press under 1 cm (½ in) around the bottom of the body.

8 Draw around the base template onto the remaining piece of cotton fabric and cut out the shape. Iron fusible webbing onto the remaining piece of calico. Trim the template down to the dotted line. Lay the template on the calico and cut out the shape. Peel the backing off the webbing and iron the calico centrally onto the fabric base. Turn the edges of the fabric over the calico, pleating the fabric neatly around the curves, and baste in place. Press the fabric.

9 Starting at one corner, ladder stitch (see page 11) the base to the front of the dress, taking the needle through the very edge of the base and the edge of the fold around the bottom of the dress. Stuff (see page 19) the head and body (the knitting needle will be useful again here), then ladder stitch the other side of the base in place. Remove the basting.

10 Slip stitch (see page 11) the trim in place around the neck and the bottom of the dress. Make hair with a fringe and side parting (see pages 17–18) from the yellow and brown stranded embroidery threads. Using backstitch, sew the hair down around the head at ear level. Work a row of chain stitch in green around the head over the line of backstitches to make a band holding the hair in place.

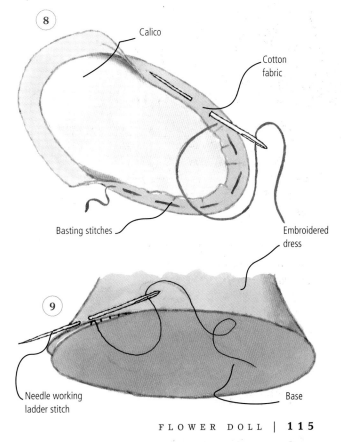

(8)

Calico

Cotton fabric

Basting stitches

Embroidered dress

(9)

Needle working ladder stitch

Base

TEMPLATES

Glove puppets (page 22)

Play cubes (page 28)

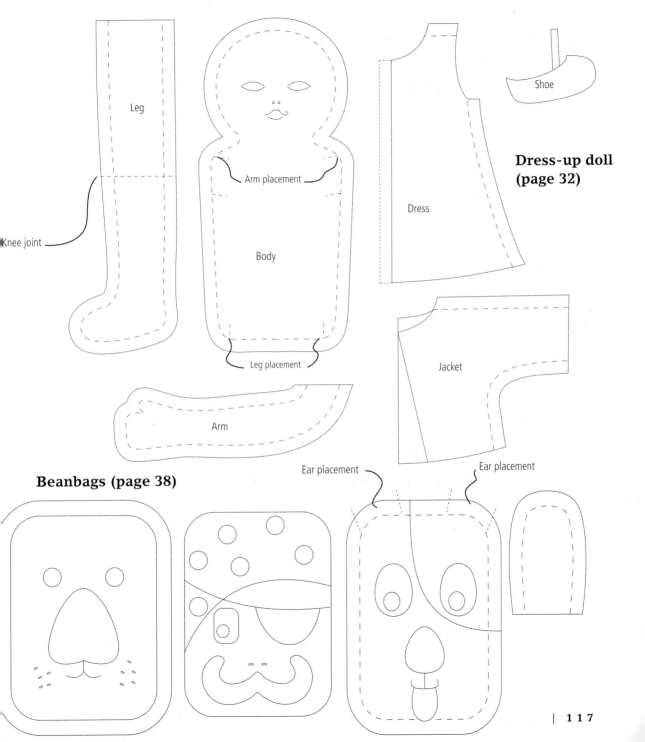

Leg

Knee joint

Arm placement

Body

Leg placement

Arm

Dress-up doll (page 32)

Shoe

Dress

Jacket

Ear placement

Ear placement

Beanbags (page 38)

Three mice (page 44)

Pocket doll (page 48)

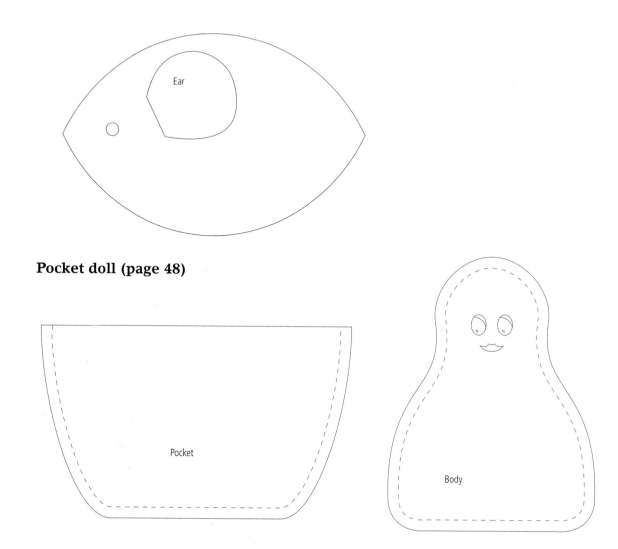

Ear

Pocket

Body

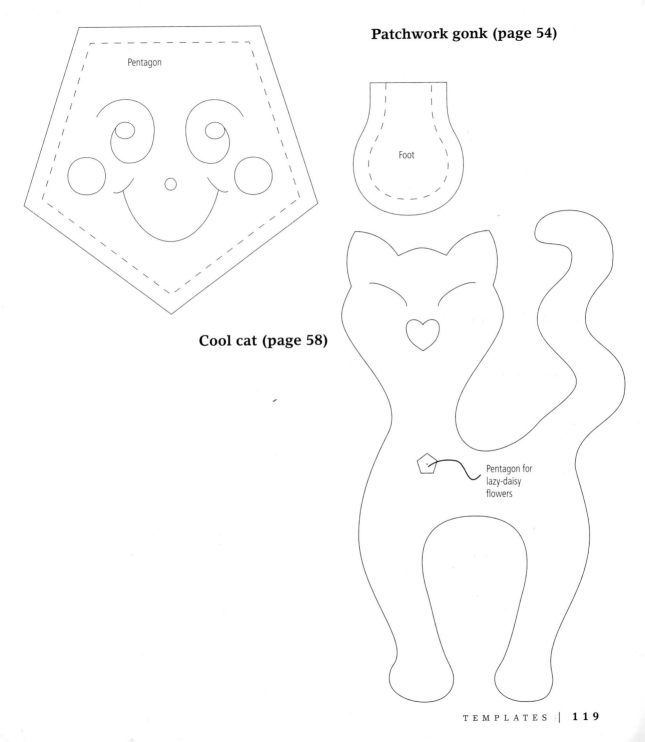

Patchwork gonk (page 54)

Pentagon

Foot

Cool cat (page 58)

Pentagon for
lazy-daisy
flowers

Quilted snail (page 62)

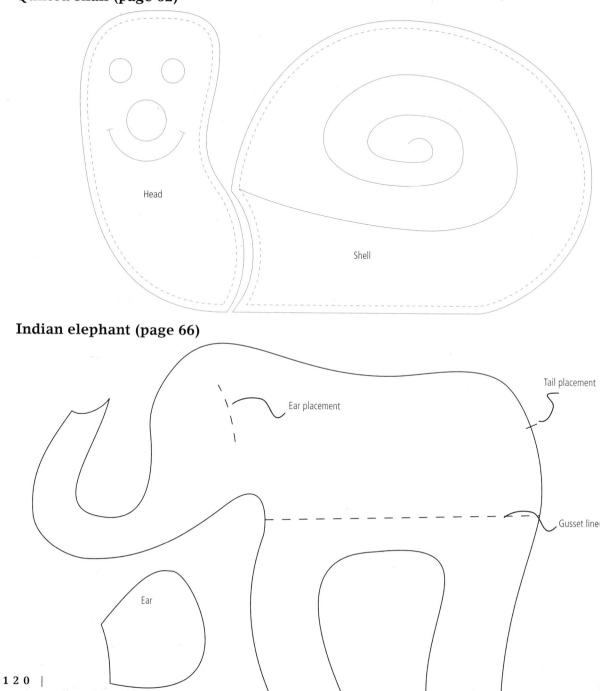

Head

Shell

Indian elephant (page 66)

Tail placement

Ear placement

Gusset line

Ear

Crazy tortoise (page 70)

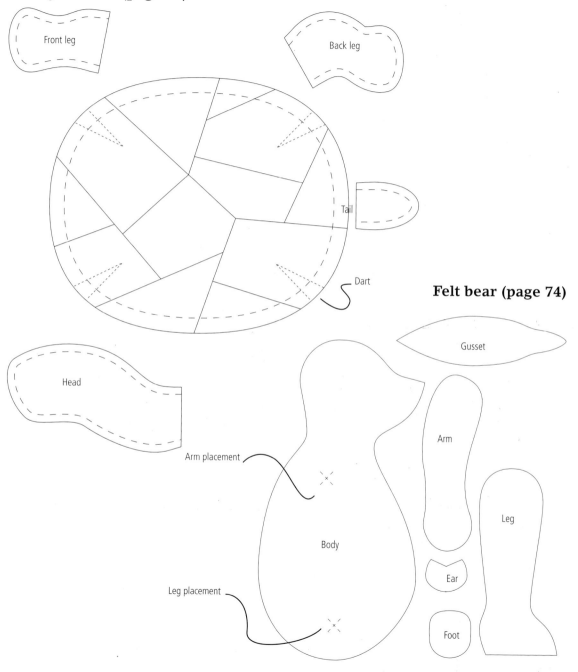

Front leg

Back leg

Tail

Dart

Felt bear (page 74)

Gusset

Head

Arm

Body

Leg

Ear

Arm placement

Leg placement

Foot

Rag doll (page 78)

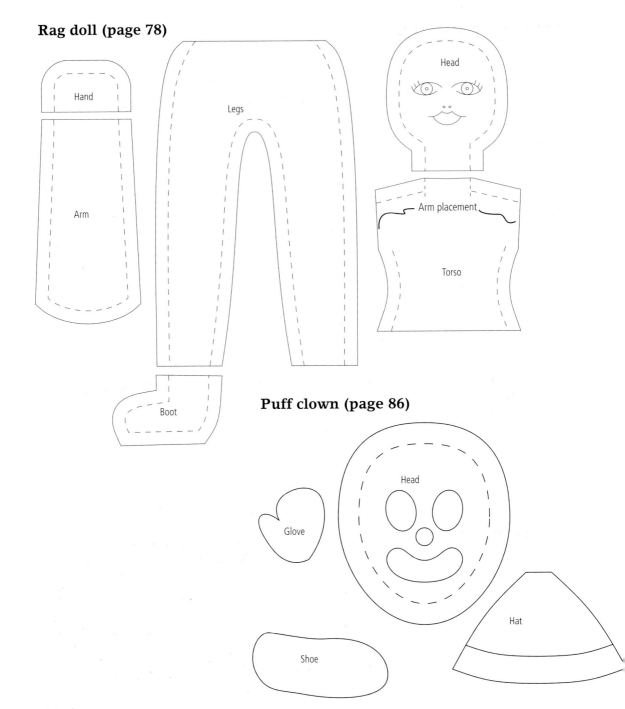

Hand

Arm

Legs

Head

Arm placement

Torso

Boot

Puff clown (page 86)

Glove

Head

Shoe

Hat

Rabbit PJ case (page 92)

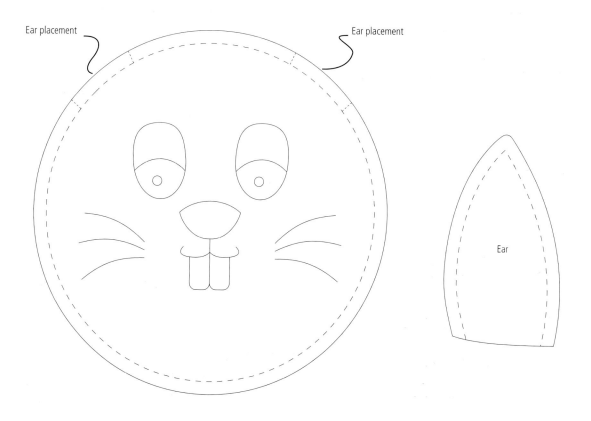

Ear placement

Ear placement

Ear

Stripy snake (page 96)

Tail

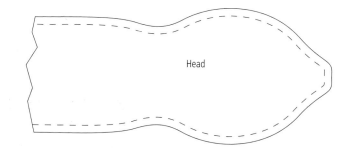

Head

Ocean liner (page 100)

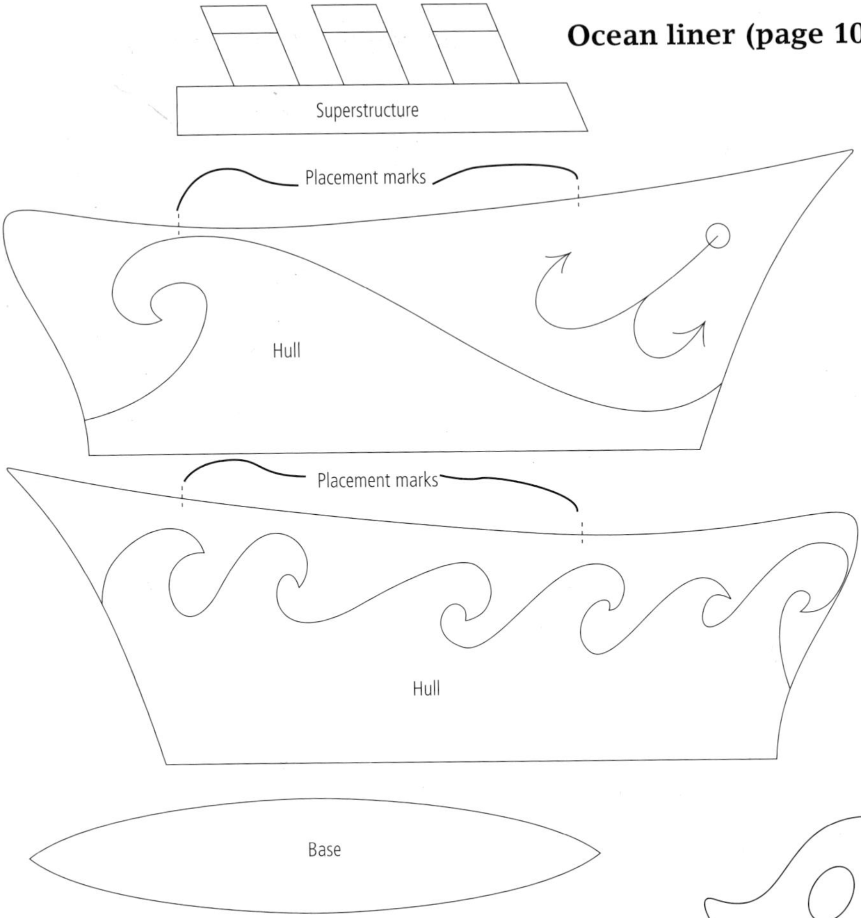

Superstructure

Placement marks

Hull

Placement marks

Hull

Base

Cute duck (page 104)

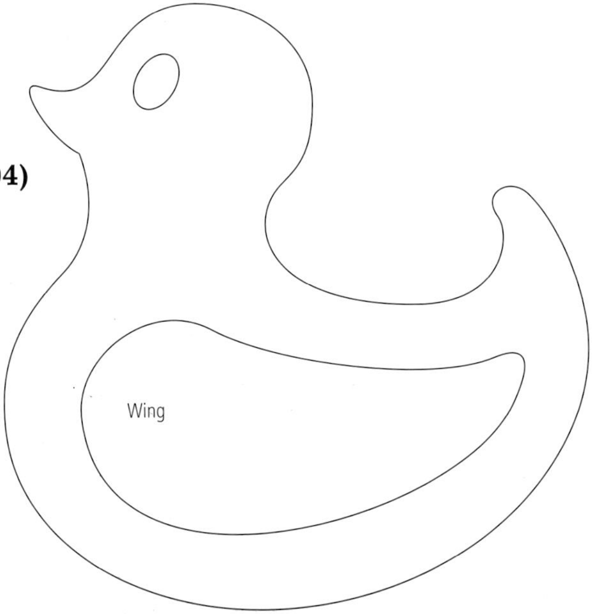

Wing

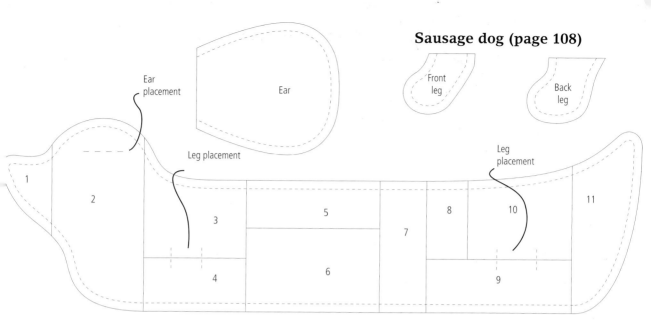

Sausage dog (page 108)

Ear placement

Ear

Front leg

Back leg

Leg placement

Leg placement

1

2

3

4

5

6

7

8

9

10

11

Flower doll (page 112)

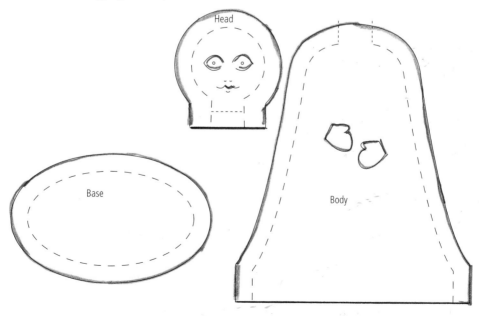

Head

Base

Body

INDEX

SUPPLIERS

CHEAP FABRICS
www.cheapfabrics.co.uk
An excellent way of buying fabrics at good prices

CLOTH HOUSE
www.clothhouse.com
Highly recommended; sells a minimum of 50 cm
(20 in) of a fabric

COTTON PATCH
www.cottonpatch.co.uk
Fat quarters and great sewing kit

JOHN LEWIS
www.johnlewis.com
First stop for sewing kit

KLEIN'S
www.kleins.co.uk
Lots of sewing kit; wide range of trimmings and
embellishments

LIBERTY
www.liberty.co.uk
Traditional fabrics; Rowan patchwork fabrics; some
other ranges

LONDON BEAD COMPANY/DELICATE STITCHES
www.londonbeadco.co.uk
Fabulous range of beads and embroidery threads

MACCULLOCH AND WALLIS
http://www.macculloch-wallis.co.uk/
Great trimmings; range of fabrics

RAG RESCUE
www.ragrescue.co.uk
Wonderful things to buy

VV ROULEAUX
www.vvrouleaux.com
Emporium of ribbons, trimmings and embellishments

ACKNOWLEDGEMENTS

My thanks to Katy Denny for commissioning this
book, allowing me to play with fabrics without feel-
ing guilty about not working, and to the team at
Hamlyn for their support. Thanks to Vanessa Davies
for the lovely photographs and Miranda Harvey for
the great book design. Kate Simunek's illustrations
are, as ever, an informative delight. And once again,
many thanks to Philip for useful suggestions, help
with templates and for feeding me.

Executive editor Katy Denny
Editor Kerenza Swift
Executive art editor Penny Stock
Designer Miranda Harvey
Production manager Linda Parry
Illustrator Kate Simunek

COMMISSIONED PHOTOGRAPHY

© Octopus Publishing Group Limited/
Vanessa Davies